Foreword

Commercial aviation is an essential part of the human planet. It transports people and goods, brings together families and friends, links cultures and societies, and helps economies to function.

Airliners provide countless connections internationally and locally. They might take holidaymakers from a rain-lashed UK to the Mediterranean or shuttle travellers between America's east and west coasts. They might ferry cargo between Asia and the Persian Gulf or provide lifeline links in the tropical Pacific or frozen Arctic.

A range of aircraft is used in commercial aviation. There are the very largest twin-aisle widebody airliners, the 'heavies', such as the Airbus A380, Boeing 747-8, Airbus A350, and Boeing 777 able to heave passengers and freight across the thousands of miles between continents. Then there are huge numbers of single-aisle narrowbody airliners such as the A320 and 737. These aircraft undertake the bulk of flying at airports throughout Europe, North and South America, Asia-Pacific and Africa.

There are the airliners sized somewhere in between the largest heavies and the single aisles, like the 787 Dreamliner and A330neo. Then there are relatively small aircraft such as the A220 and the jet and turboprop types used for regional flights.

Any airline, whatever its size or the markets it serves, wants the best possible aircraft carrying the right amounts of passengers and cargo for their needs, and which are safe, reliable, and efficient. Civil aviation is therefore always evolving.

This publication aims to provide a snapshot of the air transport industry in the mid-2020s. It looks in detail at many of the new commercial aircraft in operation today or in development, profiling some of their key features and exploring how they are used.

Considerable innovation in aircraft, engines and systems have led to strides forward in efficiency and performance since the turn of the century. All-new aircraft such as the A220, A350 and 787 have arrived and significant upgrades have been made to types like the A320, 737, A330, 777 and E-Jets.

Today, aviation is under far greater environmental scrutiny than ever before. This is spurring innovation in engines, sustainable aviation fuels, and aerodynamic technologies. Futuristic concepts for entirely new designs including hydrogen and electric aircraft have emerged. The form of new airliners is likely to change as the 21st century continues.

As this updated edition of a 2023 publication notes, the industry is grappling with persistent supply-chain challenges affecting aircraft production. Aircraft deliveries and major programmes have been delayed. Even so, the ultimate benefit commercial air travel provides will endure – connecting the world.

Mark Broadbent
Editor

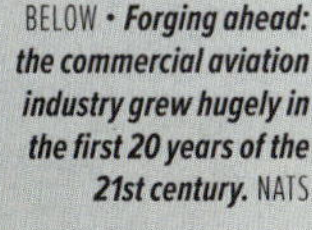

Contents

MARIAN LOCKHART/BOEING

38

PAUL WEATHERMAN/BOEING

70

AIRBUS

26

104

BOEING

EMBRAER

86

AIRBUS

98

ISBN: 978 1 83632 117 0
Editor: Mark Broadbent
Senior editor, specials: Roger Mortimer
Email: roger.mortimer@keypublishing.com
Cover design: Steve Donovan
Design: SJmagic DESIGN SERVICES, India
Advertising Sales Manager: Sam Clark
Email: sam.clark@keypublishing.com
Tel: 01780 755131
Advertising Production: Becky Antoniades
Email: rebecca.antoniades@keypublishing.com

SUBSCRIPTION/MAIL ORDER
Key Publishing Ltd, PO Box 300, Stamford, Lincs, PE9 1NA
Tel: 01780 480404
Subscriptions email: subs@keypublishing.com
Mail Order email: orders@keypublishing.com
Website: www.keypublishing.com/shop

PUBLISHING
Group CEO: Adrian Cox
Publisher: Steve O'Hara
Published by
Key Publishing Ltd, PO Box 100, Stamford, Lincs, PE9 1XQ
Tel: 01780 755131 Website: www.keypublishing.com

PRINTING
Precision Colour Printing Ltd, Haldane,
Halesfield 1, Telford, Shropshire. TF7 4QQ

DISTRIBUTION
Seymour Distribution Ltd, 2 Poultry Avenue, London, EC1A 9PU
Enquiries Line: 02074 294000.

Big picture

Highly capable new aircraft and wider changes driving the industry mean civil aviation has evolved in the past 20 years.

Civil aviation deepened its role in global trade, travel, and society during the first two decades of the 21st century. Increasing numbers of people took to the skies. International Civil Aviation Organization (ICAO) data shows there were 1.6billion air passengers in 2000. Further increases saw two billion fliers by 2006, three billion by 2013 and 4.5 billion by 2019. Put simply, nearly three times as many people were flying in the 2020s than two decades earlier.

There was more air cargo too. ICAO figures show there were 118,257 million tonnes per kilometre of air freight (a measure of the number of goods transported by air) in 2000. There were 221,096 million tonnes/km in 2019.

Then came the COVID-19 pandemic. Growth shuddered to a halt, leaving empty skies, thousands of grounded aircraft, eerie empty airports, laid-off staff, and the closure of innumerable economic, social, and cultural links. ICAO results show passenger numbers sank to 1.77 billion in 2020 – actually still more fliers in the year than at the start of the century, but down markedly on the huge figures in the 2010s.

The severe disruption from the pandemic was only part of the turbulence that hit commercial aviation in the early 21st century. A succession of geopolitical and economic headwinds buffeted the industry – the effects of the dotcom bubble bursting, the 9/11 terrorist attacks, the 2003 Iraq War, the 2008/09 global financial crisis, the 2010 Icelandic volcano eruption, fluctuating oil prices and the Russia/Ukraine war.

Through the ups and downs various airliners have arrived large, small, or somewhere in between.

New generation

The commercial aircraft market is split into several segments. At the lower end in terms of aircraft size are regional turboprops (such as ATRs) and jets (like Embraer E-Jets). Further up the size scale are the single-aisle or narrowbody twin-jets: the Airbus A220 and A320 and Boeing 737.

Next are the large widebody twin-aisle airliners, starting with the small to medium-sized widebodies with 200 to 300 seats: the A330, 787-8 and 787-9. Above them are the larger 300-to-350 seaters, the A350-900 and 787-10. The very largest airliners at the top of the market are those with 350 to 400 seats or more: the A350-1000, 777-300ER, 777X and A380.

Equipped with efficient turbofan engines and made from advanced materials, the aircraft in each of these segments – whether entirely 'clean sheet' designs such as the A350 and 787 or new versions of already established types such as the A330 and 777 – have lower operating costs and

ABOVE • *The A380 was only produced for 12 years as efficient twin-jets dominated widebody airliner sales.* P PIGEYRE/AIRBUS

ABOVE • *The Boeing 787 Dreamliner spearheaded the arrival of a new generation of efficient twin-jet airliners.* BOEING

RIGHT • *Airbus launched the A320neo Family, powered by new-generation turbofan engines, in 2010.* H JANSSEN/AIRBUS

performance efficiencies compared to earlier aircraft.

The new widebody twin-jets have been transformational. Historically, a very large four-engine quad-jet or three-engine tri-jet was required to fly lots of people over long distances. The Boeing 747, McDonnell Douglas DC-10 and MD-11, Lockheed TriStar, and Airbus A340 were examples.

No longer. Airframe and engine technology evolution means today's widebody twin-jets combine extensive range and payload with the efficiency of two rather than three or four engines. Manufacturers and airlines quote double-digit savings for their widebodies.

There has been great success for the Boeing 777 and Airbus A350. By September 2023 Boeing had received more than 2,100 orders for all Triple Seven family variants and Airbus more than 1,000 for the A350. Though slightly smaller in capacity, the 787 Dreamliner and A330 have done well too; Boeing had sold more than 1,000 787s and Airbus more than 1,800 A330s (including the first-generation variants) by the same point.

In its 2022 Commercial Market Outlook (CMO), Boeing said smaller widebodies now make up two-thirds of the world's in-service airliner fleet. Larger types have declined from 30% of the global fleet to less than 5% in the last three decades, it added.

End of the quad-jets

The fundamental shift led directly to the most notable development in the commercial aircraft scene in the 21st century so far – the two major manufacturers axing their flagship quad-jets.

Airbus made headlines at the start of the century in launching the A380. The double-deck airliner, widely dubbed the 'super jumbo', entered service in 2007 but production ended only 12 years later. Just 251 examples were sold, mostly to just one operator. Airbus had in 2011 called time on the A340 less than a decade after introducing the updated A340-500/-600 variants (the company sold just 131 examples).

The widespread adoption of capable and efficient twins also meant the Boeing 747 – for decades the epitome of long-haul, high-capacity air transport – also faced the final curtain. Boeing sold only 155 of the 747-8 variant it launched in 2005 and the company produced the last Jumbo in 2022. Twin-jet times took the quad-jets away.

New connections

The superior economics of aircraft like the A350 and 777 let airlines link major hubs cost effectively and profitably operate city pairs between hubs and airports with slightly smaller passenger numbers (known as 'secondary' destinations in industry jargon) that were previously unviable.

In the 21st century's first two decades, airlines opened 1,020 entirely new route-pairings between countries and 551 intercontinental routes, Airbus said in its 2023-2042 Global Market Forecast.

Emirates, Qatar Airways and Etihad Airways, collectively known as the 'big three' Gulf carriers, helped drive the expansion as they took an increasingly large role in global air transport. They opened dozens of routes to points in Europe, Asia, North America, the Americas, and Africa from their respective home hubs in Dubai, Doha, and Abu Dhabi.

Numerous other large airlines put the new twin-jets' capabilities to good use. British Airways deployed 777s, 787s and A350s from London/Heathrow to various cities in North America and Asia. BA's sister carrier Iberia made the A350 the backbone of its long-haul fleet serving its extensive network connecting Europe and Latin America. China Southern Airlines and Xiamen Airlines have used 787s to open routes from

RIGHT • *The Boeing 737 MAX, pictured here during flight testing, is one of the lynchpin of airlines flying short/medium-haul services.* BOEING

secondary destinations in China to Europe and Australia.

American Airlines, Delta Air Lines and United Airlines – the three US 'majors' left after the US airline consolidation in the early 21st century that saw the names of Northwest Airlines and US Airways pass into history – use 787s, A350s and 777s on their extensive global networks.

The twins enabled carriers in other markets to expand. Low-cost long-haul operators including Norse Atlantic Airways operate 787s while AirAsia and Jetstar Airways have A330s. Leisure carriers re-equipped too, TUI taking 787s and Condor A330neos.

Budget airlines

Single-aisle narrowbody airliners account for 60% of the industry's total growth, Boeing said in its 2022 CMO.

During the 2010s Airbus and Boeing launched more fuel efficient and environmentally friendly versions of their respective short-haul airliners in the form of the A320neo (new engine option) and 737 MAX.

The spectacular growth of low-cost carriers boosted single-aisle numbers early in the 21st century. A320 and 737 family aircraft are the lynchpin of budget airline operations worldwide – from Ryanair, easyJet and Wizz Air in Europe, and Frontier Airlines, Southwest Airlines and Spirit Airlines in the United States, to AirAsia and IndiGo in Asia and Azul and JetSMART in Latin America.

Budget airlines' expansion was fuelled by the liberalisation of air travel arrangements in domestic markets and improving living standards and disposable incomes spurring travel demand. Low-cost carriers, in parallel with rapidly developing e-commerce, sparked the 'unbundling' of ticket and travel options and in-flight amenities for passengers – and new opportunities for airlines to create what the industry calls ancillary revenues.

ABOVE • *Airbus had sold more than 1,300 A350s by September 2023.* B VAN DER BEEK/AIRBUS

The low-cost air travel boom created the most significant and lasting impact of 21st century aviation – the fact that it is now routine, not exceptional, for more people to fly.

New spheres

Seat numbers are a cornerstone of airline economics. Airlines risk losing money on a route if there are too many or missing out on growth if there aren't enough.

Economic trends, consumer demand, seasonality, slots, opportunities, and competition are among the many considerations for airlines when planning route networks and service frequencies.

Airlines routinely change the specific aircraft type and schedules on a route as circumstances change ('right sizing' is the industry term). This is why manufacturers have different variants of the same aircraft model offering a complementary spread of performance capabilities.

Carriers flying long-haul, for instance, might use a 787 or A330 to try out a new route before adding more capacity with a larger 777 or A350 if justified. Alternatively, if there's not enough

demand for a larger aircraft a slightly smaller-capacity yet still capable 787 or A330 enables the route to continue cost effectively. In short-haul markets, an operator might use baseline A320s or 737s but switch to the larger-capacity family variant to capture demand, or vice-versa.

The evolution of commercial aircraft during the 21st century continues to bring change. The latest single-aisle narrowbodies mean airlines that historically fly shorter-haul have been able to move into new spheres. To give a few examples, JetBlue Airways uses A321s to fly from New York to Europe, Icelandair and WestJet use 737 MAXes across the Atlantic, Air Baltic flies A220s from Riga to Abu Dhabi and Wizz Air is planning to link Europe and the Middle East with A321s.

Evolution is continuing. Boeing in its 2023-2042 CMO said: "Exiting the pandemic, many airlines are assessing their future networks and simplifying their fleet to improve operations and reduce costs."

The CMO said 75 carriers have phased out at least one aircraft type since 2019: "Airlines are increasingly focused on versatility in their widebody

BELOW • *Gulf carriers helped drive air transport expansion through the Middle East hubs.* DUBAI AIRPORTS

fleets. Key components are network flexibility, performance capabilities and efficiency across a range of routes and payload requirements."

Bouncing back

International Air Transport Association data from March 2025 shows global passenger traffic for 2024 (measured by revenue passenger kilometres) was 3.8% above that of 2019, the last full pre-pandemic year now used as a statistical baseline.

According to the 2024-2043 Boeing CMO: "The global airline network is back to 2019 levels and has adapted to new market trends."

Air travel bouncing back to the long-term growth pattern prompted an aircraft-buying spree. Orders were placed for more than 1,200 new airliners during the June 2023 Paris Air Show. Manufacturers have received so many orders that airliner production slots are fully booked to the late 2020s.

John Plueger, chief executive officer of the lessor Air Lease, told the *Financial Times* in June 2023: "It's hard to recall a time when we've had the level of demand for aircraft that we have today."

The two major manufacturers are confident about the future. Boeing's 2024-2043 CMO estimates the total commercial aircraft fleet will grow from

24,510 aircraft in 2023 to 50,170 aircraft over the next 20 years. Airbus' latest Global Market Forecast (GMF) predicts 42,230 new aircraft by 2043.

Challenges

Aviation is under mounting pressure to decarbonise. In 2022 the industry committed to achieving 'net zero' carbon emissions by 2050 under obligations ratified by the International Civil Aviation Organization. Adopting the latest aircraft, expanding efficient operations, embracing sustainable aviation fuels, and developing entirely new airframe and engine technologies are all on the agenda.

Airbus says in its 2023 GMF that the resulting sustainability push means "the pace of fleet renewal towards the most fuel-efficient aircraft will likely accelerate." There is scope to do more; Airbus said only 25% of commercial aircraft currently in service are the latest-generation aircraft.

Another pressing issue is tackling the serious supply-chain disruption that has affected the industry since 2021/22 due to shortages in raw materials and components and labour constraints. *Reuters*

reported in 2024 that while supply-chain strains were starting to ease, lead times remain long and prices remain high, and that it could take a couple more years to fully resolve the disruption.

Picking up the pace of airliner deliveries and the inherent unpredictability of the geopolitical and economic big picture (the impact of new US trade tariffs became a further concern in 2025) are all ongoing issues.

Airbus said in its 2023 GMF: "Aviation connects communities. It supports 87 million direct and indirect jobs and contributes 4.1% of global GDP." China and India continue as engine-rooms driving growth through increased trade and expanding middle classes with a desire to travel and more means to do so.

The 2022 Boeing CMO reflected: "Air travel is largely motivated by other desires: to complete a business deal, to meet with distant colleagues, to visit families and friends, to experience different places and cultures, or to relax in a beautiful location." Simply, the CMO said, "air travel is a key component of our modern world."

Only certain airliners really make people stop and look twice. Concorde could and the Boeing 747 does. With its twin decks, four engines and huge wings, the Airbus A380 is another.

The European jet is the largest, heaviest, and highest-capacity passenger aircraft currently flying. It's long as two blue whales and about as tall as five giraffes stood on top of one another. Each A380 has more than four million parts. If all the wiring on just a single aircraft was laid out end-to-end it would stretch for 320 miles, the distance from London to Edinburgh.

Singapore Airlines conducted the first A380 revenue flights on October 25, 2007. The type has completed over 800,000 commercial flights, amassed 7.4 million flying hours, and flown more than 3,000 million nautical miles, the equivalent of flying around Earth more than 125,000 times.

More than 400 million passengers have flown aboard A380s, and the type currently operates to more than 70 destinations. Airbus' official orders and deliveries statistics show that as of September 2023 there were 232 A380s in operation worldwide.

Early years

The A380 was the 21st century's first all-new commercial airliner, although its origins date back to the A3XX twin-deck concept publicly disclosed in 1994. At that time, Airbus envisaged a launch in 1997/98 and service entry in 2003/04.

In the end, the A380 was formally launched on December 19, 2000. Initial prototype F-WWOW (c/n 1) rolled out at Toulouse-Blagnac Airport on January 18, 2005, and flew on April 27, 2005. European Union Aviation Safety Agency and US Federal Aviation Administration type certifications were received on December 12, 2006.

Issues with the aircraft's electrical wiring disrupted early production. Wiring harnesses on each aircraft had to be replaced – an issue complicated by the A380's sheer physical size and an ambitious development timetable where customisation and production ramp-up occurred in parallel.

Airbus ended up reducing production rates during 2007-09 and revising delivery schedules. A plan to develop an A380 freighter variant provisionally ordered by FedEx and UPS was put on indefinite hold (it was never revived).

There was further disruption during 2012 after hairline cracks were discovered in the wings of Qantas Airways and Singapore Airlines A380s. Airbus changed the assembly process and retrofitted all A380s with a thicker, stronger alloy.

Luxury in the air

Back in the mid-1990s when the A380 was still at the A3XX concept stage, an Airbus ad about the then-still prospective super jumbo was shown on European and North American TV channels. The ad asked if some of the Seven Wonders of the World had a cinema, a casino, and a gym – a peg on which hung the line, 'You'll find all these things on the Airbus A3XX, where wonders never cease'.

No A380s ever received those particular features, but certain operators did introduce other 'wonders' mentioned in the ad, including a spa and bedrooms. In its marketing for the aircraft Airbus claims the A380 offers "the best cabin in the sky" and a "unique passenger experience."

BELOW • *Emirates operates more A380s than any other airline with 123 in service as of mid-2023.* EMIRATES

A380

Europe's super jumbo is now out of production, but it remains an important aircraft for the airlines flying it.

ABOVE • *Various operators suspended A380 operations have returned their super jumbos to service as air travel demand increased after COVID-19.* ETIHAD AIRWAYS

The A380's two decks provide 550m² of useable floor space (50% more than a Boeing 747-400). Airbus says the main deck cabin is the widest of any airliner. There is capacity for up to 545 seats in a standard four-class configuration "with no compromise on comfort," according to Airbus, although most examples have between 450 and 520 seats.

Individual airlines configure their A380s differently and have invested in lavish first and business class products. The United Arab Emirates flag carrier Etihad Airways has a unique A380 cabin offering with The Residence, a private suite at the front of the upper deck of the aircraft designed for two guests with a living room, bedroom, and en-suite bathroom.

Emirates, Etihad Airways, Qantas Airways, Singapore Airlines and Asiana A380s have fully-enclosed first-class suites. Other operators do not but nevertheless offer spacious facilities. First class on British Airways A380s, for instance, has 14 open suites with the seats having a 180° lie-flat recline.

Emirates' jets have a shower/spa for all first-class passengers. Most A380s have an onboard bar and lounge area for first class/business passengers. In economy class a 31-34in seat pitch is typical.

Onboard cameras enable passengers to see the views ahead, beneath the aircraft and from the top of the tailfin on their in-flight entertainment screens as the A380 flies along, bringing a unique

BELOW • *An Emirates A380 leads the Fursan Al Emarate, the UAE Air Force Aerobatic Team, at the 2018 Dubai Airshow.* AIRBUS

perspective to take-off and landing especially. The cabin features LED mood lighting with changing colours at different times of day and HEPA (High Efficiency Particulate Arrestor) air filters. The entire cabin air is fully refreshed every two to three minutes. There are 15 different temperature control zones in the cabin and the temperature in each zone can be varied between 18°C and 30°C.

Airlines always seek to improve the in-flight experience and A380 cabins have evolved. In 2017 Singapore Airlines introduced a 471-seat interior with a new premium class and more business-class seats. Qantas was the launch customer for Cabin-Flex, a new 11-abreast economy seat layout on the main deck that replaces the forward staircase connecting the main and upper decks with an aft straight/square module to create space for more seats.

Where do A380s fly?

The A380's seating capacity obviously makes it ideal for serving airports with large passenger numbers so inevitably the type is a familiar sight at the largest hub airports including Dubai, London/ Heathrow, Frankfurt, Hong Kong, Singapore, Dallas/Fort Worth and Los Angeles.

Emirates operates far more A380s than any other operator (123 aircraft as of May 2025). The super jumbo is intrinsic to the Gulf airline's business model, where spokes extend from its Dubai hub to a dense network

Airbus A380 operators

All Nippon Airlines, Asiana Airlines, British Airways, Emirates, Etihad Airways, Korean Air Lines, Lufthansa, Qantas Airways, Qatar Airways, Singapore Airlines

Data correct to May 2025. N.B. list does not include former operators Air France, China Southern Airlines. Global Airlines plans to start operations in 2025.

ABOVE • *An Etihad Airways A380 flights at London/ Heathrow in July 2023 after arriving from Abu Dhabi.* ETIHAD AIRWAYS

A gust load alleviation system detects airflow changes ahead of the aircraft and automatically deflects the ailerons upwards in turbulent conditions to distribute gusts across the wingspan to minimise drag and smoothen the ride.

A380s are powered either by Rolls-Royce Trent 900 or Engine Alliance GP7200 engines. A Trent 900 enhanced performance package introduced elliptical leading edges to the engine blades to improve efficiency and the GP7200 received engine control software improvements.

Airbus' in-house FAST publication lists various other innovations. Structural reinforcements increased payload/range capability; operators can choose from 13 different weight variants ranging up to 575,000kg maximum take-off weight. Aluminium-lithium composites introduced on the lower wing skin save weight and metallic components were improved to increase fatigue strength.

of destinations worldwide. Emirates flies A380s not only to large hubs but also 'secondary' airports: destinations with smaller passenger numbers than the biggest hubs but still with sizeable traffic.

In 2021, Emirates' president Sir Tim Clark told a *Simple Flying* webinar: "The power of the hub allows us to take these flights. One [A380] flight will feed 80 destinations within two hours of arriving. You can imagine the incremental revenue that we gain at incremental cost. As the hub gets larger its unit costs fall and its income generation rises exponentially."

This does not necessarily mean the A380 is well suited to all routes. London/Heathrow-New York/JFK might seem tailor-made for the aircraft owing to the numbers of people flying it; the latest Civil Aviation Authority figures show there were 3.2 million passengers in 2024.

However, British Airways has never used A380s on the route, instead using Boeing 777-300ERs and 787s. A characteristic of the market is passenger preference for multiple departures all day, so it makes more commercial sense to run several daily frequencies using slightly smaller aircraft rather than an A380 to fly lots of people in one go.

Nevertheless, the ability to fly large passenger numbers in a single movement by A380 is useful at slot-constrained hubs to maximise seat capacity, freeing slots to do something else and/or add more seats to a route.

Aircraft evolution

The A380 has received various airframe and systems upgrades. Airbus introduced a wing twist of 1.5° in 2010 to improve the wing's profile during flight and reduce fuel burn ('twist' refers to the position of the tip relative to the root).

Flight deck

The A380's cockpit has eight 5.9in x 7.8in interactive displays: two for primary flight information, two for navigation, one for engine parameters, one for systems and two that can be customised to the pilots' preferences.

Head-up displays show critical flight information symbols in the pilots' forward field of view. Live pictures streamed from the external nose and tailfin cameras displayed on one of the screens assist the flight crew with ground steering. A graphical representation of airport runways and taxiways helps with ground navigation.

Directly above the LCD screens are the autopilot, speed, direction, and altitude controls. On the ceiling panel above the crew hydraulics, electrics, fuel pumps,

RIGHT • *Big in Japan: All Nippon Airways A380s wear a distinctive turtle design livery.* H GOUSSÉ/AIRBUS

air conditioning, pressurisation, and fire systems controls.

The central console between the pilots' seats is home to the navigation and communication buttons. The crew use a keyboard control unit and a track-ball cursor to manipulate the flight management systems; each pilot also has their own keyboard on a pull-out tray.

A380s have sidestick control columns, as with all other Airbus aircraft. Pilots transition between the A380 and other Airbus aircraft via a Cross-Crew-Qualification highlighting systems and handling variations.

Brake-to-Vacate lets pilots select a specific runway exit while the aircraft, with auto-flight, auto-brake and flight controls regulating deceleration after touchdown to reach the specified exit at the optimum speed. There is a Runway Overrun Protection system.

The A380 has a paperless cockpit. Flight maps, navigation, airport charts and technological manuals are displayed electronically on an Onboard Information System which collects, centralises, and compiles all the data related to the flight. Up to a million aircraft performance parameters are tracked with over 100 different maintenance reports generated for condition monitoring and fault reporting.

An updated data system automatically displays and backs up airspeed and altitude data. Autopilot/flight director traffic collision and avoidance system (TCAS) combines the autopilot, flight director and TCAS to provide a vertical speed guidance to create optimum avoidance manoeuvres from conflicting air traffic. A new TCAS Alert Prevention mode reduces TCAS Resolution Advisory warnings during a level-off manoeuvre.

Airbus A380 seat numbers

All Nippon Airlines	480
Asiana Airlines	495
British Airways	469
Emirates	489, 517 or 615 depending on configuration
Etihad Airways	490
Korean Air Lines	407 or 399 depending on configuration
Lufthansa	509
Qantas Airways	484
Qatar Airways	514
Singapore Airlines	471

Data correct to September 2023.

At airports

Airbus says more than 400 airports worldwide are A380-compatible. Airports require 60m-wide runways, 25m-wide taxiways and a minimum 

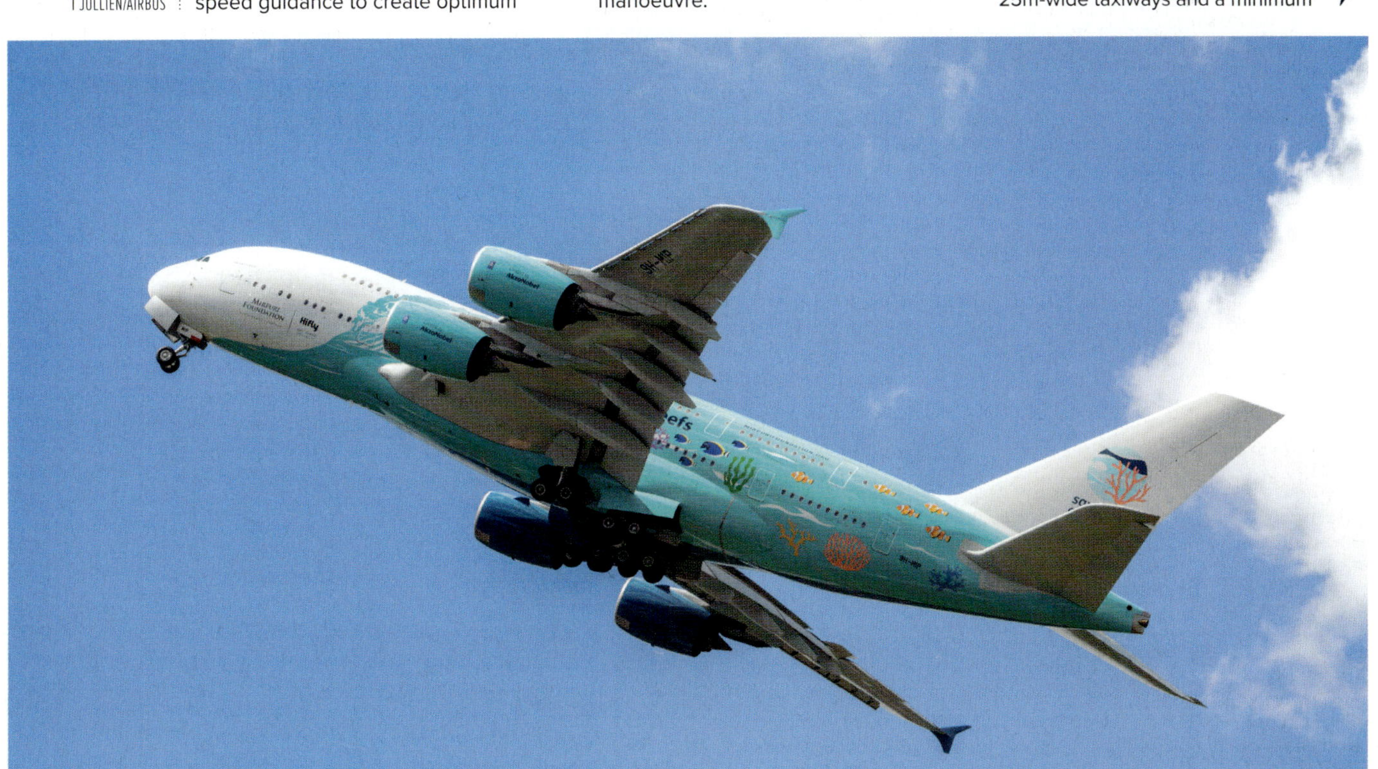

From the cockpit
First Officer Alex Orchard, Emirates

Q) How would you sum up the A380?
"The Emirates A380 is the most iconic and recognisable aircraft in the world and getting to fly it is one of the biggest perks of my job. The wealth of technology on board, its spacious interior and Rolls-Royce Trent 900 engines make it a hugely comfortable and smooth travel experience for both passengers and pilots. For such a large aircraft, people are often surprised at how quiet the A380 is while in the air."

Q) What most impresses you about the aircraft's performance?
"The A380 is a dream to fly. There is a tremendous amount of engineering and technological know-how that enables such a large aircraft to operate at a low noise level with such smooth motion and a 70,000lbf thrust capability. The aircraft not only has the biggest passenger capacity with space for 615 seats on our two-class configuration, but it also has one of the longest ranges in the world and can travel up to 15,000km in one journey."

Q) What are the most significant features of the flight deck?
"The spacious cockpit provides seating for flight crew with space for flight bags and much more. The layout of all the systems has been carefully designed by Airbus and by working closely with Emirates over the years, they have produced an ergonomically flawless machine. With keyboards integrated into the tray tables and an innovative track ball mouse design for use on the screens, it is easily noticeable how this aircraft is a product of the 21st century.

"With operating such a large aircraft across many different airports around the world, the Emirates A380 must be able to deal with a whole range of challenges on a day-to-day basis. The aircraft benefits from a vast array of protections that help pilots avoid hazardous situations and maintain its record as one of the safest aircraft in commercial aviation. These protections work both in the air but also on the ground, using automation alongside pilot inputs to operate at peak safety and efficiency levels.

"One system we use most days is Brake-to-Vacate, an automated braking system which allows the selection of the exact point on any runway that the pilots wish to stop or vacate by. While boasting a fantastic safety record, the aircraft is also impressive in performance. The wing is almost 80m in diameter, combining that with four powerful Rolls-Royce engines and you can effortlessly lift 575 tonnes of passengers and machinery into the air!."

Q) How would you rate the A380 among other types you have flown?
"I have flown several different aircraft throughout my career before joining Emirates, from gliders and small piston aircraft to the A320. It has been a privilege to experience them all. I can confidently say, however, that the A380 tops that list. The A380 simply excels in multiple areas. It is larger, faster, and safer – a genuine pleasure to fly, from the front and also to experience in the back.

The Emirates A380s operate to many diverse locations across our global network of over 130 destinations, so you get to travel extensively across the world, explore lots of new countries and cultures and meet new people along the way. A certain standout moment in my memory was the first time I sat in the right-hand seat of the A380. After all the preparation and training you receive from the company, nothing can ready you for the excitement and adrenaline rush of doing your first take-off and landing.

"Flying is more than just a job for me, it has been my passion for decades. I know there are many others out there interested in joining Emirates to experience this. If you are willing to accept the challenge and chase that dream, I guarantee you will not be disappointed. This job, operating the Emirates A380, is truly unique."

ABOVE • *A British Airways A380 above the White Cliffs of Dover.* BRITISH AIRWAYS

57.5m clearance to ground objects under International Civil Aviation Organization (ICAO) Aerodrome Reference Codes.

Various improvements were made ahead of the A380's service entry. Runways, taxiways, and aprons were widened and reinforced, lighting and signage repositioned, and new air passenger boarding bridges (APBBs) were installed. Departure and arrivals halls, baggage carousels, customs and security facilities and retail/refreshment outlets were upgraded.

Emirates' large fleet brought major changes at Dubai International. Concourse A, opened in January 2013, was the first purpose-built A380 terminal with 20 contact gates and 13 remote stands. Each gate has triple APBBs (two connected to the lower deck and the third to the top deck).

There are also triple bridges at Heathrow, Frankfurt, Los Angeles, and Singapore. Specialist catering trucks with longer scissor lifts are required to access the aircraft's upper deck, 26ft above the ramp and specialist four-wheel drive ground vehicles to the aircraft on the apron.

In ICAO terminology the A380 sits in its own 'Super heavy' class. Air traffic controllers enforce wider separation to aircraft following behind: it's six nautical miles for 'heavy' widebody airliners (aircraft with a 305,000lb maximum take-off weight), rising to 7nm separation to 'medium' types (e.g., A330s) and 8nm to 'light' types (A320s, 737s, regional jets). A heavy taking off behind an A380 is held for three minutes; it's four minutes if the next departure is a medium or light type.

A380s axed…

In the 2000s/2010s the annual Airbus Global Market Forecast consistently predicted demand in the very large aircraft (VLA) segment of the market where the A380 sits. Long-term growth in passenger numbers and capacity constraints would make higher-capacity aircraft inevitable, the company said. Its 2019 forecast, for example, envisaged 1,184 VLA sales out to 2036.

The pace of super jumbo sales, however, was in realty sluggish at best. Emirates placed its last firm A380 order in 2013. Air France and Qantas Airways

ABOVE RIGHT • *First and last: the very first A380 (left) faces the final production example at Toulouse in 2021.* L BORCK/AIRBUS

cancelled provisional repeat orders and Hong Kong Airways and Virgin Atlantic Airways scrapped purchase plans. A declining backlog meant Airbus scaled back annual output from a peak of 30 jets in 2014 to eight in 2019.

A lessor called Amedeo placed a provisional order for 20 in 2014 but those aircraft were never delivered. Portuguese carrier Hi Fly in 2017 took on a single ex-Singapore Airlines A380 (9H-MIP c/n 6) for wet-leasing but only operated the aircraft for three years.

Airbus unveiled a package of proposed improvements in 2017 called A380plus including the Cabin-Flex seating, drag-reducing winglets, and further performance increases. Emirates' Sir Tim Clark urged Airbus to go further and develop an A380neo (new engine option) with more efficient turbofans.

Neither A380plus nor A380neo happened. The persistent lack of interest in the aircraft, and ultimately Emirates revising its long-term Airbus fleet plans and ordering A350-900s, led to an inevitable conclusion. On February 14, 2019, Airbus announced it would stop making the A380. The company delivered the last new example (A6-EVS c/n 272) to Emirates in December 2021.

Tom Enders, Airbus' chief executive officer when the decision to end production was made, commented: "It was painful to take the decision after all the effort, money and sweat our employees have poured into that programme, but we have to base on decisions on facts."

Crucially, while the A380s fits various high-volume markets, there are ultimately only so many routes where so many seats are required. And having so many seats in a four-engine aircraft meant the A380's economics paled against those of the widebody twin-jets. In total, Airbus only sold 251 A380s.

Tellingly, most operators have limited super jumbos compared to those other widebody aircraft. Here are a few examples (figures as of May 2025). British Airways has 12 A380s but it also has 18 A350-1000s, 42 777-200ERs, 16 777-300ERs, 12 787-8s, 18 787-9s and ten 787-10s. Qantas has ten A380s but it uses 26 A330s and 14 787-9s and has ordered A350s. Lufthansa has eight

RIGHT • *An A380 was the first Emirates aircraft to be repainted in the latest version of the carrier's livery.* EMIRATES

ABOVE • *The A380's cockpit has eight 5.9in x 7.8in interactive displays.* NICK MORRISH/BRITISH AIRWAYS

A380s but it also uses 30 A350s and it has ordered 34 787-9s. Singapore Airlines has 12 A380s, but the carrier operates 63 A350-900s, 26 777s and 19 787s.

...and return

The severe air travel downturn caused by COVID-19 grounded A380s. Air France, China Southern Airlines and Malaysia Airlines subsequently phased out their A380s permanently.

In 2021 both Etihad Airways and Lufthansa said they did not plan to return their examples to service and Thai Airways International is looking to dispose of its six examples it put into storage.

Air travel's recovery following COVID-19, however, has meant A380s have returned to the airways as airlines seek to maximise seat numbers to cater for resurgent demand. Qatar Airways restored eight of its ten aircraft in service as of mid-2023 (although the carrier still plans to phase out its aircraft by 2028 as new Boeing 777-9s arrive). Etihad resumed A380 operations on July 25, 2023. Its aircraft only served its Abu Dhabi-Heathrow initially, but the carrier has since restored the type to its services to New York/JFK, Mumbai, Paris/CDG and, in February 2025, Singapore. Emirates has restored A380s to multiple routes in the extensive network from its Dubai hub in recent years, to points in Europe, Asia and North America. Copenhagen, Munich and Prague are the latest Emirates A380 routes in summer 2025.

Qantas restored A380s to some of its Melbourne-Los Angeles frequencies in 2023. It also flies the aircraft to Johannesburg and Singapore, and in August 2025 will open a new Sydney-Dallas/Fort Worth route.

Lufthansa A380s currently operate between Munich and Boston, Denver, Los Angeles, New Delhi, New York, and Washington, DC. British Airways uses its superjumbos from Heathrow to Boston, Johannesburg, Los Angeles, Miami, San Francisco, Singapore and Washington, DC.

A start-up UK airline has turned to the A380. Global Airlines went public in spring 2023 with plans to "reinvigorate the flying experience, courtesy of the unrivalled spaciousness offered by the super jumbo."

Airbus A380 basic characteristics

Wingspan	79.7m (260ft 9in)
Length	72.7m (238ft 6in)
Height	24.1m (79ft 4in)
Wing area	845m²
Maximum fuel capacity	320,000 litres (84,535 US gal)
Maximum take-off weight	480,000kg (1,058,259lb) to 575,000kg (1,267,58lb)
Seats	555 standard but variable according to customer, maximum certified capacity 868
Cruise speed	Mach 0.85
Maximum range	8,478nm (15,700km)
Engines	4x Rolls-Royce Trent 900s or Engine Alliance GP7200s generating 70,000lbf (311kN) thrust

Data: Airbus

ABOVE • *The bedroom in The Residence, the three-room suite at the front of the top deck on Etihad Airways A380s.* ETIHAD AIRWAYS

ABOVE RIGHT • *Emirates' ghaf tree motif and hand-stencilled panels in the first-class shower spa of the carrier's latest A380 cabin upgrade.* EMIRATES

BELOW • *Dubai Airport's Concourse A was the first purpose-built A380 terminal.* EMIRATES

The company is working with authorities and partners to launch transatlantic flights in spring 2025. It has an agreement with Hi Fly to agreement with Hi Fly "to work together on the development and maintenance of the four A380 aircraft the new airline has agreed to acquire."

Global's first A380, on the Maltese civil aircraft register as 9H-GLOBL, is a former China Southern aircraft. Global's first A380 service was be a charter flight from Glasgow International Airport, Scotland to New York/JFK on May 15, 2025, followed by a charter flight from Manchester to New York/JFK, on May 21, 2025.

'A new standard'

A380 production ending less than 20 years into the aircraft's operational career marked a line in the sand for commercial aviation: the type will likely be the last new large passenger airliner with four engines thanks to twin-jet efficiencies.

Airbus says its aircraft development programmes "have benefited from the many innovations and processes developed with the A380." The A350's gust load alleviation system, flightdeck technologies and onboard data management were all developed on the A380 first, for example.

Airbus claims in its marketing the A380 "opened a new standard in aviation" for passengers. Operators continue to invest in A380 cabins. Emirates has introduced a refreshed interior including 56 premium economy-class seats and improved first and business classes. Sixty-seven jets will receive the refurbishment. Lufthansa will install its latest Allegris business-class cabin from 2024 and British Airways intends to retrofit its examples with its latest first-class and Club Suites (the new business class).

The A380 continues to offer airlines utility for handling capacity pressures and accommodating demand on popular routes. Airbus says the type "will continue flying, with Airbus support, for decades to come" and promises further improvements for the in-service fleet.

Emirates' president Sir Tim Clark continues to call for a re-engine. During the 2023 Paris Air Forum, a pre-Paris Air Show conference, he claimed using the Rolls-Royce UltraFan turbofan would give "startlingly good" 25% reductions in fuel burn and emissions.

The A380 remains popular with travellers. Clark told the Paris Air Forum there was an 82% load factor on Emirates A380s in spring 2023. The Gulf airline plans to continue flying A380s well into the 2030s.

Clark told the 2021 IATA World Air Transport Summit: "The notion that the technocrats, the accountants who all say this aircraft is not fit for its purpose, it is environmentally unfriendly, etcetera…doesn't resonate with our travelling public. They absolutely love that aeroplane."

747

The last Boeing 747 was handed over to its customer in early 2023, ending half a century of jumbo production.

The 747 is an icon of 20th century aviation but it remains firmly part of the story with the 747-8.

Boeing developed two new variants of the classic airliner in the 21st century – the 747-8 Intercontinental passenger version (747-8I) and the 747-8 Freighter (747-8F) – but this latest iteration of the jumbo could not resist the wholesale change in the commercial aircraft market to smaller, efficient, and highly-capable twin-jet airliners.

Sluggish sales meant that on July 29, 2020, Boeing announced it would stop building the 747-8 after completing the assembly and delivery of the orders then remaining in the backlog. This would end a continuous production run lasting half a century.

The very last new 747 (N863GT c/n 67150) – the 1,574th jumbo – rolled out from Boeing's factory at Everett north of Seattle in December 2022. The aircraft was handed over in February 2023 to Atlas Air, which operates the aircraft for Apex Logistics.

Jet age

Boeing turning out the last new 747 truly was an end-of-an-era moment in commercial aviation. The 747 was not the first long-haul jetliner – that was the De Havilland Comet back in the 1950s – but the jumbo symbolised the growth of mass air travel in the second half of the 20th century that made aviation a fixture in the developed world.

Indeed, the 747 emerged in response to the burgeoning market created by the Comet and the Boeing 707 and Douglas DC-8 which followed. In the mid-Sixties, Juan Trippe, the president of Pan American Airways, one of Boeing's most important airline customers, wanted a larger aircraft. Trippe personally asked Bill Allen, Boeing's chief at the time, to develop a jetliner two and half times the size of the 707 that could carry more passengers and thereby offer a 30% lower cost per unit of passenger-distance.

RIGHT • Boeing 747-8 Intercontinental N6067U, later N828BA (c/n 37826), is pictured back in 2013 test-flying a performance improvement package. This aircraft is now stored. BOEING

BELOW • With 28 examples UPS Airlines operates more Boeing 747-8s than any other carrier. UPS AIRLINES

Boeing launched the 747 programme on April 13, 1966; Pan Am ordered 25 examples. The first 747-100 rolled out at Everett on September 30, 1968 and undertook its first flight on February 9, 1969. Boeing handed over the first aircraft to Pan Am on December 3, 1969 with the airline beginning its first route with the aircraft, New York/JFK-London/Heathrow, on January 22, 1970.

Airlines quickly saw the potential the widebody twin-aisle 747 offered. In the 1970s and 1980s the aircraft joined the fleets of operators worldwide, from major network airlines to independent carriers such as Branff and Virgin Atlantic Airways.

The 747 helped to open entirely new leisure and business travel markets, and the passenger numbers the aircraft brought encouraged airport infrastructure developments. The jumbo family evolved further with the 747-200, 747-300 and 747-400 variants.

The 747 took jet air travel into a different league. It was the first large twin-aisle widebody airliner and was instrumental in making possible the mass air travel boom from the 1970s. Some say the aircraft even changed perceptions about air travel.

Richard Voss, director of Ignite Architects, reflected in a blog: "Even though you might not be flying first class across the Atlantic, by the mere fact that you were in a jumbo jet, you were associated with a new luxury in air travel. It infused a layer of glamour, which had not been previously experienced by airline passengers en-masse."

By 1984 the 747 was used for 60% of all flights across the Atlantic operated by US airlines and by 1997 for 80% of US carriers' services across the Pacific Ocean to Tokyo/Narita Airport in Japan, according to a 2003 presentation by Boeing to the International Civil Aviation Organization

The 747's dominance of long-haul flying was not to last thanks to the rise of the efficient twin-engine widebody airliners, led by the jumbo's own Boeing stablemate, the 777. With two fewer turbofan engines, extensive range and plentiful underfloor revenue cargo capacity, the twin-jets do much of what the 747 can do, but more efficiently. The 'Queen of the Skies' became yesterday's aircraft.

In that same 2003 presentation to ICAO, Boeing itself reported the jumbo's use by US airlines on transatlantic passenger flights had sharply decreased from the early-1980s high of 60% to just 4% by the early 2000s. The type's usage on those transpacific services between the US and Tokyo/Narita had dropped too, from 80% in 1997 to 60% in 2001.

Heavyweight

Such was the way the wind was blowing that in hindsight it might seem surprising Boeing decided to launch the 'Dash Eight' jumbo at all. The company did however need a presence at the top of the widebody aircraft market for the highest-capacity passenger aircraft to counter Airbus and its A380, launched in 2005.

Boeing had explored various development options for the jumbo in the late 1990s and early 2000s, including the 747-500X/-600X proposals of 1996 and the subsequent 747X Stretch to enable the type to carry 400-500 passengers.

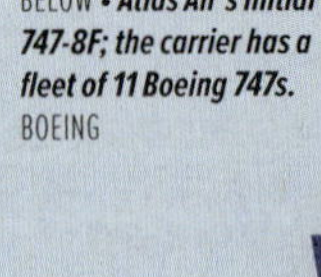

BELOW • *Atlas Air's initial 747-8F; the carrier has a fleet of 11 Boeing 747s.*
BOEING

Boeing 747-8 Freighter basic characteristics	
Length	250ft 2in (76.3m)
Wingspan	224ft 5in (68.4m)
Height	63ft 6in (19.4m)
Maximum fuel capacity	59,734 US gal (226,095 litres)
Maximum take-off weight	987,000lb (447,700kg)
Total cargo volume	30,288ft³ (857m³)
Cargo positions	34 main deck, 12 lower deck
Cruise speed	Mach 0.85
Range	4,200nm (7,778km)
Engines	4x General Electric GEnx GE-2B67 engines, each generating 66,500lbf (296kN) maximum take-off thrust

Data: Boeing

Some of the 747X Stretch ideas ended up in the 747-400 Extended Range and 747-400ERF Extended Range Freighter subvariants Boeing launched in 2000/01. Qantas Airways took on six 747-400ERs and Air France Cargo was the initial 747-400ERF operator in 2002.

Boeing launched the 747-8 programme on November 14, 2005. Production work on the initial 747-8F began in 2008 and the aircraft undertook its first flight on February 8, 2010. The second example flew on March 15, 2010 and the third two days later. The fourth example (the first for initial 747-8F operator Cargolux) joined the test fleet on July 23, 2010 and a fifth on February 3, 2011. The first 747-8I passenger variant flew on March 20, 2011; it was later joined by two further test aircraft.

The US Federal Aviation Administration and European Union Aviation Safety Agency type-certified the 747-8F on August 19, 2011; Cargolux accepted its first aircraft two months later. 'Type cert' for the 747-8I followed in December 2011 and Lufthansa introduced the aircraft in June 2012.

The 747 is a 'heavy' – the term in air traffic control radio transmissions indicating that controllers must put extra distance behind an aircraft to minimise wake turbulence for aircraft following behind. (Under the US Federal Aviation Administration's classification, 'heavy' specifically refers to airliners with a maximum take-off weight of 305,000lb or more.)

And the 747-8 is among the heaviest of the heavies. At 250ft 2in in length it is the longest 747 ever produced; the previous-generation 747-400 is 231ft 10in long. The 747-8 is not quite as lengthy as was the solitary 84m-long Antonov An-225, destroyed in Kyiv, Ukraine in February 2022.

The 747-8 is also slightly shorter than the 251ft 9in-long 777-9, its latest Boeing stablemate, but it is longer than the A380.

ABOVE • *The very last new jumbo built, 747-8F N863GT (c/n 67150) – the 1,574th example of the type – was handed over in February 2023 to customer Atlas Air, which operates the aircraft for Apex Logistics.* BOEING

The 747-8's 987,000lb maximum take-off weight is higher than the 747-400's 875,000lb but lower than the A380's.

'Just looks right'

The 747 always makes for an imposing sight thanks to its size and distinctive profile of its characteristic humpback fuselage, four large engines and swept wings.

BELOW • *A UPS 747-8F over the Rockies. The aircraft can transport large payloads over more than 4,000nm.* BOEING

Mark Vanhoenacker is a Senior First Officer for British Airways who flew the 747-400 for 11 years. He is the author of the critically-acclaimed books *Skyfaring* and *Imagine a City*.

In *Skyfaring*, Vanhoenacker wrote: "Partisans often say that the 747 'just looks right'. I agree, but this isn't necessarily what you'd think of a plane with such an unnatural 'bump'…The

> ### Boeing 747-8 operators
>
> Air Belgium (for Hongyuan Group), Air China, AirBridgeCargo, Apex Logistics (operated by Atlas), Atlas Air, Brunei Government, Cargolux, Cathay Pacific Cargo, Egypt Government, Government of South Korea, Korean Air, Korean Air Cargo, Kuehne+Nagel (operated by Atlas), Lufthansa, Morocco Government, Nippon Cargo Airlines, Royal Flight of Oman, Polar Air Cargo, Qatar Airways Cargo, Qatar Emiri Flight, Silk Way West Airlines, State of Kuwait, Turkey Government, UPS Airlines.
>
> Data correct to September 2023.

lines of the 747 may be so satisfying not despite the nose bump, but because of it."

In *Skyfaring* Vanhoenacker reflected that the 747 "possesses the scale of a structure or enclosure we might inhabit." Decades earlier, the aircraft's designer Joe Sutter declared his aircraft was "a place, not a conveyance" and the British architect Sir Norman Foster once proclaimed the jumbo as the 20th century 'building' he admired the most.

In the 1991 BBC TV series 'Building Sights', Foster explained: "It has style associated with cultural ideas of speed, efficiency, power, strength and dependability – and yet it is genuinely beautiful. I believe all modern architecture must be capable of this intrinsic style and beauty without in any way compromising its function."

Perhaps only an architect could describe an aircraft in these terms, but the point is the 747 truly has a presence and an aura. The 747 compels whether you are standing beside it, flying aboard it, watching it taxi, take off or land.

It even does so from a distance. This publication's editor recalls as a child in the 1990s on clear days watching, through binoculars, airliners leaving contrails high above northern England on blue-sky days as they started their descents into Heathrow. It was always a buzz when, looking through the binoculars, you saw it was a 747.

The type achieved a rare feat for an airliner – truly widespread public recognition. So much so, indeed, that it even features in songs. 'Take a jumbo/across the water' sang Supertramp in *Breakfast in America*. 'Glide like a 747' goes a lyric in *Let's Groove* by Earth, Wind and Fire. 'Got on board

Second lives

Despite the diminishing role for the 747-400 during the early 21st century as a passenger airliner, dozens remain active as freighters including converted ex-passenger examples. Some 747-400s have also found second lives in more specialist roles.

Boeing operates four examples of an extensively modified 747-400 variant known as the Dreamlifter to transport subassemblies for the 787 Dreamliner between subcontractors' facilities and its final assembly sites.

Rolls-Royce acquired former Qantas Airways 747-400 VH-OJU (c/n 25566) in October 2019 to become a flying testbed for new turbofan engines. The aircraft is currently undergoing conversion by AeroTEC facility in Moses Lake, Washington. In an industry first, this jumbo will be configured to test both commercial airliner and business aircraft powerplants.

More spectacularly, a jumbo once used by Virgin Atlantic Airways has dropped space rockets. The former G-VWOW (c/n 32745) was converted into a platform for Virgin Orbit. Reregistered N744VG and named *Cosmic Girl*, the 747 lifted the LauncherOne rocket under its port wing to high altitude. From there the rocket was released to climb into Low Earth Orbit and launch satellites.

Cosmic Girl first launched a rocket over the Pacific Ocean in May 2020. A second launch in January 2021 delivered tiny satellites called CubeSats to orbit and four subsequent launches in 2021/22 succeeded. A launch of commercial payloads in January 2023, with the aircraft operating from Cornwall Newquay Airport, failed after the rocket suffered a post-release engine thrust malfunction.

Virgin Orbit subsequently entered US bankruptcy protection in a bid to find new investors. These could not be secured and so Virgin Orbit's assets were put up for sale. In May 2023 it was announced the technology company Stratolaunch had received US Bankruptcy Court approval to acquire the 747 to add further capacity for air-launching vehicles, including the Talon-A hypersonic testbed. Stratolaunch operates the unique Scaled Composites 351 carrier aircraft (N351SL) and is based at Mojave Air and Space Port, California.

ABOVE • *Ground support and cargo handling equipment for the 747-8 is the same as the 747-400 to maximise commonality.* UPS AIRLINES

a westbound Seven Forty-Seven' sang Albert Hammond in *It Never Rains in Southern California.*

'Come and gone'

The 747 may well be a pop-culture icon, but the aircraft's place as a mainstay of the world's airways slowly but surely became a thing of the past during the early 21st century.

According to data published in January 2023 by the IBA consultancy, there were around 1,000 active and operational 747s worldwide back in 1998. Year-on-year decreases in fleet numbers meant that by the start of 2023 there were 346 active examples of all jumbo variants left in operation, IBA said. The 747's

time, a December 2022 *Forbes* article remarked, "has come and gone."

IBA observed the 747's lifecycle "has followed a broadly typical profile" of any ageing airliner – a parallel decrease in active fleet numbers and increase in retirements – but it pointed out the 747 fleet "was notably hit by the Coronavirus pandemic."

The retirement of older 747-400s was very much under way when COVID-19 started to impact the industry early in 2020, but the pandemic sped up the withdrawal process. British Airways, KLM Royal Dutch Airlines, Lufthansa, Qantas Airways, Virgin Atlantic Airways and the French leisure airline Corsair were among the operators to

immediately ground their remaining 747-400s and send them to storage when the pandemic struck.

Lufthansa brought back some 747-400s but many others did not return. Qantas and Corsair bade farewell to their last 747s in spring/summer 2020; KLM and BA followed suit in October 2020. Retired 747s ended up in storage at various locations – in Spain at Castellón, Cuidad and Teruel airports, in the US at Kansas City, Mojave, San Bernardino, Victorville and Pinal Air Park, and in the UK at Cotswold Airport (Kemble), Newquay and St Athan.

Several retired 747s were later scrapped, including some of those that ended up at Kemble and St Athan. A few found new operators but others have joined the ranks of retired airliners stored forlornly in quiet desert boneyards, lifeless relics of past times.

High-capacity hauling

The changeover to the twin-jets was further illustrated by the lack of 747-8 sales: Boeing sold just 155 examples before the decision in 2020 to axe the type as a current-production model.

There were just 47 examples built of the 747-8 Intercontinental passenger version. Air China (seven), Lufthansa (19) and Korean Air (ten) are the only commercial airlines flying it; the rest are business jets or used by governments.

Most 747-8s (107 aircraft) are freighters. Major cargo carriers all operate the

LEFT • *Cargolux uses 16 747-8Fs. The upwards-swinging nose cargo door is a distinctive sign of the freighter jumbo's loading flexibility.* BOEING

aircraft, including UPS Airlines (28), Atlas Air (11), Cargolux (16), Cathay Pacific Cargo (14), Nippon Cargo Airlines (eight) and Korean Air Cargo (seven).

The 747-8F offers plentiful lift capacity, with 34 main-deck pallet positions and 12 lower-deck positions and a maximum cargo payload of 307,600lb. By comparison the 747-400F has 30 main-deck and nine lower-deck positions and 258,600lb payload.

With twice as many examples as any other carrier, UPS Airlines is the lead 747-8F operator. The Louisville, Kentucky-based carrier is set to take on a couple more second-hand examples, a March 2023 report to shareholders saying it plans to have 30 747-8Fs in service by the end of 2023.

Captain Sten Rossby, a 747 tech and safety pilot at UPS Airlines, told this publication's editor: "The 747-8F was an easy fit for UPS in many ways. We can use the same pilots, ground staff and much of the same ground handling equipment with the 747-8F and 747-400F. It provides flexibility to [scale] up and down size capacity between these two variants and not have to move crews around to cover the flights."

Capt Rossby continued: "This aircraft adds value to our operation in many ways, such as additional capacity at a lower unit cost. It can also take the same payload as a 747-400 further. It is economically and environmentally very flexible in that sense."

The 747-8F's capacity and 4,200 nautical miles range means the type is ideal for flying the long-haul trunk routes between the world's main airfreight hubs where there is the greatest need for capacity.

Taking a look at the various online flight-tracking websites shows, for instance, UPS 747-8Fs shuttling between the company's Worldport hub in Louisville to Anchorage, Cologne, Dubai, Hong Kong, Shenzen and

Taipei. The carrier also operates 747-8Fs to Bangalore, Bangkok and New Delhi.

Capt Rossby said: "The aircraft provides quite some flexibility for our route planning staff. We can use it on short domestic flights to consolidate flights on smaller jets, but also for direct flights like our daily flight to Dubai. The 747-8 adds significant extra capacity at a lower cost and carbon dioxide footprint per unit of volume."

Old and new

There are various differences between the 747-8 and its 747-400 forebear. The 'Dash Eight' has General Electric GEnx GE-2B67 engines, which according to GE's figures provide 66,500lb of maximum take-off thrust compared to the 56,400-63,300lb generated by the GE CF6, Pratt & Whitney PW4000 and Rolls-Royce RB211 engine choices on the 747-400F.

Boeing says the 747-8F burns 16% less fuel and produces 16% fewer carbon dioxide emissions compared to the 747-400F. It says the aircraft operates at 52% below International Civil Aviation Organization Committee on Aviation Environmental Protection 6 limits for nitrous oxide emissions.

The 747-8F has a new wing featuring raked tips, fly-by-wire spoilers and outboard ailerons to save weight and cut drag. Double-slotted inboard and single-slotted outboard flaps, an aileron droop and redesigned flap track fairings optimise low-speed performance and cut noise. Krueger flaps assist in low-speed handling.

Despite the engine and airframe differences, commonality with the 747-400 was a prime goal for Boeing to limit change to the spares inventory and minimise costs. Other than a larger tow bar, the ground support equipment requirements for the 747-8F such as pneumatic start carts, ground power units, portable loaders and trucks supplying electrical power, conditioned air and water, are the same as for the 747-400F.

Cargo handling equipment used on the ramp, including the hydraulic lift used to load containers and pallets, and the aircraft's internal power drive system powering the rollers that move payloads into position on the main and lower decks, is also identical to the 747-400F.

The 747-8 has the same type rating as the 747-400, even though the flightdeck has technologies brought across from the 787 Dreamliner such as multifunction displays, electronic flight bag provision, an electronic checklist, an airport moving map display, integrated approach navigation, GPS autoland, a vertical situation display and an onboard network server.

The blend of the old with some of the new minimised training requirements.

ABOVE • *At 250ft long and with a 224ft wingspan the 747-8 is the largest 747 variant.* UPS AIRLINES

BELOW • *Recent years have seen 747-400s retired by airlines including British Airways, one of whose 747-436s (G-BYGC c/n 25823) painted in a BOAC 'retrojet' livery, is pictured flying with the Red Arrows during the 2019 Royal International Air Tattoo.* CPL ASHLEY KEATES/ROYAL AIR FORCE

ABOVE • *The rise of the efficient long-haul twin-jet airliner meant the sun set on the 747 as a current-production aircraft.* LUFTHANSA

BELOW • *Some 747-400s have found niche uses; Stratolaunch plans to use the former Virgin Orbit aircraft for air-launch missions.* STRATOLAUNCH

UPS' Capt Rossby explained: "For the UPS operation, the 747-8 is flown by the same pilots as the 747-400. There is no full flight simulator or specific flight training required to fly the 747-8 once you are 747-400 qualified. A 747-400 pilot will feel very much at home in a 747-8."

Capt Rossby continued: "Prior to their first flight in a 747-8 there is some self and instructor led study. Boeing worked closely with the initial customers to ensure that each new feature that was added to the aircraft added value. Many of these new features allow for a common crew complement, yet the 747-8 is ready to support advancements of the ever changing and modernising ATC environment. The new Flight Management Computer was such an improvement that UPS took the decision to retrofit it to the 747-400 fleet. This has improved the operational flexibility of the 747-400."

Overall, Capt Rossby enthused: "Most pilots who fly the 747, love it! It is the dream of many to fly the 'Queen of the Skies'. This makes it a fairly senior aircraft for our pilots, especially for captains who want to fly her before the end of their careers.

"The crews appreciate the advanced features of the 747-8. It is a bit like upgrading to a newer version of one's favourite car. It has the same general feeling and behaviours, but is a nicer ride. There are, of course, some who prefer to fly the 'classic' 747-400."

'Changed the world'

With the 747-8F still youthful in aircraft-age terms (the oldest in service only dates back to 2011) and the last 747-8Fs off the line in 2022 still pretty much factory-fresh, the 'Dash Eight' jumbo will remain a vital cog in the global logistics machine.

Indeed, when the 747-8Fs are taken together with the older 747-400Fs still flying, the jumbo still accounted for 20% of the total cargo aircraft fleet worldwide, noted *Forbes*' December 2022 analysis.

The 747-8 is also the basis for the next-generation aircraft for the US Air Force's presidential air transport mission. (Any aircraft carrying the US President uses the callsign 'Air Force One' when the President is aboard.)

A pair of converted 747-8Is are undergoing conversion to VC-25Bs. The extensive modifications include power upgrades and the installation of communications, avionics and self-defence systems. These aircraft are expected to enter service from 2026, succeeding the current VC-25As (converted 747-200s) that have been used since the 1980s.

Whether flying presidents or freight pallets, the charismatic jumbo will remain airborne for many years to come. But the last new 747 delivery is notable nevertheless – and former 747 pilot Mark Vanhoenacker is in no doubt about the type's place in history.

In 2023, he told this publication's editor: "The 747 changed the world. It democratised long-haul travel and connected people and places like no other innovation before it. Whenever I see a photo of a 747 my heart skips a beat."

Those to have flown aboard the 747, stood beside the aircraft or simply just seen it fly, might well say the same.

A350

Airbus' flagship long-haul airliner is now the A350 twin-jet, with its advanced materials, engines and systems proving popular with pilots.

Marking ten years in airline service in 2023, the A350 family had amassed 1,391 orders from 56 customers by May 2025. There were 654 examples in service with 40 different operators at that time. The type has completed more than 1.7 million revenue flights since entering service.

Airbus is developing new ultra-long-range and freighter variants. Now operated on more than 1,000 commercial air routes, the A350 will be the backbone of airline flying for years ahead.

Development

Airbus launched an initial A350 in December 2004 but, in the wake of Boeing promising big operational savings with the 787 Dreamliner launched that year, there was a muted reception from the market.

A resulting comprehensive redesign saw the A350 relaunched in 2006 as the A350 Xtra Wide Body (XWB). Three variants were planned: the baseline A350-900, a lengthened, higher-capacity A350-1000 and a shortened, longer-range A350-800 (the latter was subsequently cancelled).

The initial A350-900 (F-WXWB c/n 1) flew from Toulouse-Blagnac on June 14, 2013. Four further test aircraft followed: F-WZGG (c/n 3) on October 14, 2013, F-WWCF (c/n 2) and F-WZNW (c/n 4) on February 26, 2014 and F-WWYB (c/n 5) on June 20, 2014.

The A350-900 received European Union Aviation Safety Agency (EASA) certification on September 30, 2014 and US Federal Aviation Administration (FAA) approval on November 13, 2014. Launch operator Qatar Airways received its first aircraft (A7-ALA c/n 26) on December 22, 2014 and undertook the first intercontinental A350 service from Doha to Frankfurt on January 15, 2015.

The A350-1000 first flew on November 24, 2016. Three flight test aircraft (F-WMIL c/n 59, F-WWXL c/n 71, now Virgin Atlantic G-VDOT and F-WLXV c/n 65, now Air Carabies F-HMIL) completed a 1,600-hour flight/certification test campaign. The variant received EASA and FAA type certification on November 21, 2017. Qatar Airways introduced the aircraft on Doha-London/Heathrow on February 24, 2018.

Family members

The A350-900 is 66.8m long, seats 300-350 passengers, carries 36 LD-3 freight containers as underfloor revenue cargo, and has a baseline 8,300 nautical miles range. The A350-1000 is slightly longer (at 73.7m), seats 350-410 passengers, carries 44 LD-3s and

BELOW • *The five A350-900 flight test/ certification aircraft in formation including those in the 'carbon' livery to highlight the aircraft's extensive carbon-fibre usage.* AIRBUS

RIGHT • *F-WMIL (c/n 59), the first A350-1000 flight test aircraft, during an early flight test near the Pyrenees.* S RAMADIER/AIRBUS

has 8,700nm range. Both variants have the same 64.7m wingspan. Rolls-Royce Trent XWB-84 engines generating 84,200lb thrust equip the A350-900. Higher-rated XWB-97 turbofans (97,000lb) are used on the larger A350-1000.

The A350-1000's greater length and higher maximum take-off weight means it has a slightly larger wing area and a wing trailing-edge extension to optimise lift and cruise performance. The variant also has a six-wheel main landing gear (the A350-900's is four-wheel), a reinforced nose landing gear and slightly different flaps to cope with higher aerodynamic loads.

Wing shape affects fuel burn but the loads a wing experiences in flight also impact performance. Airbus concluded that giving the A350's wing the ability to essentially adapt its shape in flight by optimising its aerodynamic profile would help the aircraft perform as efficiently as possible.

Variable camber adapts the flaps' position and inner and outer flaps can be selected differentially as required. Adaptive flaps change the wing's trailing edge profile to control the gap between the flaps and the spoilers. There is also a gust load alleviation feature – technology originally developed for the A380 – that deploys ailerons during turbulent conditions to evenly distribute wind gusts across the wings and ensure airflow is optimal to minimise drag.

Advanced materials

Historically, most airliners were produced mainly from metallic parts. By contrast 70% of the A350 is made up of advanced materials, including carbon fibre reinforced plastic (CFRP) composites, titanium and aluminium-lithium alloys.

Materials research showed CFRP is typically 20% lighter as well as stronger and more durable than aluminium. Composites mean the features of a traditional metallic fuselage such as joints and fasteners can be removed, saving weight. Composites also mean no corrosion and fatigue tasks in maintenance activities.

Carbon fibre makes up 53% of the A350's structure including the wings, centre wing box, keel beam, tail cone, fuselage frames, panels, stringers and doublers, clips, window frames, and passenger and cargo doors. The wing box consists of single-piece CFRP top and bottom covers and front and rear CFRP spars.

From the cockpit

David Ward, A350-900 captain, Delta Air Lines

Q) How would you sum up the A350 from a pilot's perspective?
"It is a real pleasure to fly. The large windscreens on the flightdeck allow for great forward and lateral visibility, the advanced avionics and onboard information systems present flight information to the pilots, and the precise and responsive manoeuvrability of the aircraft through the sidestick controls work seamlessly to make this jet a well-behaved and fun to fly aircraft."

Q) What are the best features of the aircraft?
"There are so many enhancements on this aircraft compared to previous generations. The best features include the connected flight deck providing flight plan information wirelessly to the onboard Electronic Flight Bag [EFB], which in turn displays this information on the large format display screens for the pilot.

"The FlySmart app on the EFB displays flight plan data from the company as well as enroute maps, airport approach charts, the aircraft operational document, and performance applications required to operate the aircraft.

"Many of these apps can be controlled using the large format touchscreens, providing intuitive and quick access to the information. The system also links system discrepancies to the Equipment List in the EFB for quick reference/analysis of operations with that discrepancy.

"Another best feature of this aircraft is the 6,000ft ambient cabin altitude while at cruise altitudes. This is 1,500 to 2,000ft lower than most commercial airlines and provides an enhanced cabin experience for both our customers and our crews."

Q) What most impresses you about the aircraft's performance?
"The overall fuel efficiency of this aircraft is a real plus. The 84,000lb of thrust provided by the Rolls-Royce Trent XWB-84 engines give the jet a smooth constant cruise speed of Mach 0.85, significantly faster than many commercial airliners.

"The wing of the A350, combined with these engines, allows us to reach an initial cruise altitude 2,000ft higher than almost any other commercial airliner in production today. This higher initial cruise altitude provides greater fuel efficiency."

Q) Tell us about the flightdeck and some key features
"There are six large format display units on the flight deck. These are touchscreen capable and some of the data such as the FMS, the FlySmart on board information systems including the enroute map, airport approach charts, and company ACARS communications, may be displayed on different screens as a function of pilot/crew requirements and or phase of flight.

"There are dedicated controls and keyboards to access and control apps not accessible though the touchscreen functionality. Another key feature is its capability to automatically relocate displayed information should a display unit fail. This assures mission-critical data such as the primary flight display and navigational information are readily available in the event of a display unit failure.

"The ECAM or Electronic Centralised Aircraft Monitor System facilitates flight crew monitoring and management of aircraft systems. The ready access facilitates routine system checks and the automated selection of checklists provide crew guidance on system status and in the event of an abnormal situation. This is far superior to referencing paper checklists – it both saves times and mitigates potential human factors issues."

Q) What other systems are particularly useful?
"Brake To Vacate is an excellent operational feature. Allowing the pilots to preselect the exit point from the landing runway, the system provides automated braking modulated to slow the aircraft in the most energy dissipation efficient manner.

"This provides a smooth deceleration and saves wear and tear on the braking system while also minimising the heat build-up in the brakes themselves. Use of this system, which we use on most of our landings, combined with proper pilot taxiing techniques, virtually eliminates the concern of hot brakes in the gate area.

"The Runway Overrun Warning and Protection provide another level of safety by monitoring the computed landing distances and alerting the pilot if a potential overrun is detected both before the landing and after the aircraft has landed on the runway. This additional level of safety can help the pilot take appropriate action earlier than might otherwise be the case to prevent a runway excursion."

Q) Any other systems that stand out?
"The A350 has a harmonised approach guidance system (xLS) that uses the Instrument Landing System localiser and glideslope information where available. When these are not available the FMS and multi-mode receiver generate a pseudo localiser and glideslope for display and tracking. The generated guidance looks very much like an ILS. The control, displays and activation functions are all the same as if the approach were an actual ILS approach.

"Flight control surfaces that are electrically controlled and hydraulically actuated by one or both hydraulic systems or by an independent source provide an excellent level of redundancy.

"The ability of the flight control system to maintain any selected angle of bank less than 33° as selected by the pilot thought the sidestick control means the pilot may roll into an angle of bank and then move the control stick to neutral while the aircraft holds that angle of bank until the pilots subsequently command wings level."

Q) How would you rate the A350 among other types you have flown?
"The A350 combines composite structures, advanced efficiency engines and avionics, onboard information management systems and a pressurisation system to provide a low cabin altitude with more fresh air to perfect the art and science of air travel. Hard to beat that."

Q) Are there any particularly memorable experiences you have flying this aircraft so far?
"There are many. Greeting a young visitor to the flight deck before we take them on their journey, making landfall after 16 hours of flying almost entirely over the oceans, seeing the vast beauty of Greenland or the state of Alaska from 40,000ft and the Northern Lights over the North Pacific Ocean, and completing a mission and seeing and hearing thank you from passengers.

"On a recent flight to Tokyo, ATC directed us to hold and subsequently change the approach we would fly and the runway on which we would land. The advanced functionality of the A350 FMS allowed us to quickly reconfigure our flight plan routing to add the holding pattern and make the other changes almost effortlessly. The large-format screens made this information readable from all seats on the flight deck and the navigation display allowed us to confirm the changes made were those we intended."

ABOVE RIGHT • Delta Air Lines is one of numerous carriers to have ordered A350-900s to replace older widebodies.
DELTA AIR LINES

The A350's fuselage is made of four large CFRP panels. Airbus says in its in-house FAST technical publication that, "longer panels assembled together into four sections are considered more mature and more beneficial to aircraft than having only cylindrical sections."

All the CFRP parts are produced at Airbus' factory at Stade, Germany by laminating ribbons of carbon fibre using a tool called an Advanced Fibre Placement Machine equipped with a sophisticated control system enabling complex shapes to be created while minimising waste.

Titanium makes up 14% of the A350's structure. It is used for some high-load fuselage frames, door surrounds, engine pylons and the landing gear. Door frames are made from a CFRP/titanium hybrid.

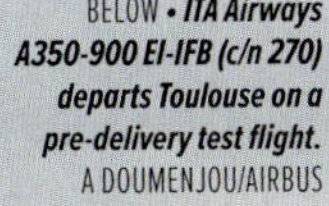

BELOW • ITA Airways A350-900 EI-IFB (c/n 270) departs Toulouse on a pre-delivery test flight.
A DOUMENJOU/AIRBUS

Integrated Modular Avionics

An important technical feature of the A350 is an Electrical Power Distribution System (EPDS), which controls the use of key functions aboard.

According to Airbus' in-house FAST technical publication, the A350 features "more use of solid-state power control technology, providing a modern method of power control management throughout the aircraft, which eliminates the need for individual circuit breakers in the cockpit, cabin and electronics bay."

The A350 has an Integrated Modular Avionics (IMA) architecture which, as the name suggests, brings together functions that would traditionally require separate units on the flightdeck. IMA governs the operation of the electrical, hydraulic, pneumatic, fuel, air conditioning and pressurisation systems, the engines, landing gears and the flight deck.

The A350 also has an Avionics Data Communication Network, which uses the Airbus-patented AFDX (Avionics Full DupleX switched) Ethernet system – initially developed for the A380 – to exchange operational and maintenance data. AFDX is designed to offer more secure and reliable communications between systems aboard because it uses Ethernet rather than physical wiring.

Initially Airbus wanted to use Lithium-ion (Li-ion) batteries on the A350 due to their greater energy density than conventional nickel cadmium batteries. It later opted to use nickel cadmium in the wake of Boeing's woes with the 787, grounded for five months in 2013 due to issues with its Li-ion battery system.

An Airbus statement at the time said nickel cadmium batteries were "proven and mastered" and

LEFT • *The A350's flight deck features large-format displays and electronic flight bag compatibility.* BRITISH AIRWAYS

Airbus A350 orders and deliveries

	Orders	Deliveries
A350-900	1,001	559
A350-1000	327	96

Source: Airbus Orders and Deliveries data, May, 2025

that using them would be "the most appropriate way forward in the interest of programme execution and reliability."

Onboard Maintenance System

The A350 has an Onboard Maintenance System. Airbus explains in FAST: "The crew is informed of functional degradations through consequential effects which will be handled at the end of the flight by a mechanic, based on their association with maintenance messages in the Post Flight Report.

"The A350 is designed in such a way that no maintenance message is triggered if no effect impacts flight, cabin or maintenance operations. This allows the maintenance staff to isolate the important fault messages and concentrate on their final troubleshooting solution using interactive links in the main maintenance technical data."

It continues: "As proved with the A380, the OMS reduces the time for fault-findings and fault-isolation, with less potential for non-routine work and with a reduction in terms of No-Fault Found removal rate."

Maintenance staff on the ground can also review the aircraft's performance in flight in real time thanks to AIRMAN (AIRcraft Maintenance ANalysis), which

further helps troubleshooting and proactive maintenance.

The A350 was the first commercial aircraft to enter service with permanent radio frequency identification tags, which enable remote reading and writing of component data. A part's complete history can be stored in detail, providing quicker and more reliable management.

Recent technical improvements to the A350 include lighter electrical, water/waste and heating systems, more composites (on wing covers, landing gears, doors and air conditioning ducts) and software changes for slat and flap positions.

Technical snags

Teething problems often affect new airliners and the A350 was no exception. Early in the aircraft's operational career

BELOW LEFT • *Lufthansa will introduce its new Allegris in-flight product on the A350 in 2024.* LUFTHANSA

BELOW RIGHT • *Rolls-Royce Trent XWBs are the sole engine available on the A350 family.* J V REYMONDON/AIRBUS

Airbus issued service bulletins for some onboard equipment and removed galley inserts (including coffee makers and ovens) because of leaks.

Software improvements had to be made to the OMS and to address overheating warnings in the bleed air system. Quality issues affected business-class seats on some customer aircraft.

In July 2019 EASA issued an Airworthiness Directive mandating A350-900 operators to turn off the power supply to their aircraft after 149 hours of continuous power-up.

This directive, to essentially reboot the A350 at a certain time interval, followed analysis of in-service events where, EASA said, "a loss of communication occurred between some avionics systems and the avionics network."

The directive said: "Depending on the affected aeroplane systems or equipment, different consequences have been observed and reported by operators, from redundancy loss to complete loss on a specific function."

Separately, in August 2021 Qatar Airways discovered degradation in the paint surface on its A350-900s. Qatar's regulator grounded the carrier's aircraft until the root cause could be determined. The carrier stopped accepting deliveries and on December 20, 2021, Airbus received a formal legal claim in the UK High Court filed by Qatar Airways relating to the issue.

A trial was set for summer 2023 but in February 2023 the two parties announced an "amicable and mutually agreeable settlement" had been reached. An Airbus statement said: "A repair project is now underway and both parties look forward to getting these aircraft safely back in the air."

Airspace

Airbus created an all-new cabin for the A350 called Airspace which the manufacturer claims "is the quietest

ABOVE • *Air France's initial A350-900 F-HTYA (c/n 331) captured during a pre-delivery test flight out of Toulouse.* P MASCLET/AIRBUS

LEFT • *The Loft aboard Virgin Atlantic A350s.* AIRBUS

BELOW • *Delta Air Lines has used the A350 to replace older Boeing 777s.* DELTA AIR LINES

Airbus A350 basic characteristics

	A350-900	A350-1000
Wingspan	64.75m (212ft 5in)	64.75m (212ft 5in)
Length	66.80m (219ft 2in)	73.78m (242ft 4in)
Height	17.05m (55ft 11in)	17.08m (56ft)
Maximum take-off weight	283,000kg (623,908lb)	319,000kg (703,274lb)
Maximum fuel capacity	141,000 litres (37,248 US gal) or 165,000 litres (43,588 US gal) on ULR	159,000 litres (42,003 US gal)
Cargo capacity	36 LD3 containers or 11 pallets	44 LD3 containers or 14 pallets
Seats	300-350 in three class (440 maximum)	350-410 in three class (480 maximum)
Cruise speed	Mach 0.85	Mach 0.85
Maximum range	8,300nm (15,400km)	8,700nm (16,100km)
Engines	2x Rolls-Royce Trent XWB-84s with 84,000lbf (?) thrust	2x Rolls-Royce Trent XWB-97s with 97,000lbf thrust

Data: Airbus

area called The Loft for its aircraft. Meanwhile, Lufthansa has announced its A350s will be the first aircraft to be equipped with the carrier's new Allegris cabin from 2024.

How are A350s used?

The A350 has replaced various earlier-generation widebodies such as Boeing 747s (as at British Airways and Virgin Atlantic), Airbus A340s (Finnair and Lufthansa) and older Boeing 777s (Delta Air Lines and Singapore Airlines).

Airbus says the A350 provides a 25% advantage in fuel burn, carbon dioxide emissions and operating costs compared to previous-generation aircraft in its size class.

Airbus says the A350 offers flexibility and efficiency for all market segments. Large airlines like to operate aircraft with varying seat counts so they can account for changing demand and 'right size' the capacity they provide.

The A350 is a useful tool in a carrier's network-planning armoury, enabling an operator to add capacity to a long-haul route if required or try out a new route with less risk than using a slightly higher-capacity aircraft.

For the likes of Singapore Airlines, Qatar Airways, Etihad Airways, Delta Air Lines and British Airways, the A350 complements other widebody equipment, from slightly smaller 787s to larger 777s and A380s in some cases.

Going further

Airlines' requirement for flexible aircraft able to do different tasks means manufacturers develop different capabilities for their designs.

LEFT • *The Airbus A350-1000 has six-wheel main landing gears, made by Safran Landing Systems.* S RAMADIER/AIRBUS

BELOW • *The Luftwaffe (German Air Force) uses a VIP-configured A350 for VIP transport.* S KRUIJER/AIRBUS

of any twin-aisle and offers passengers and crew the most modern in-flight products for the most comfortable flying experience."

The aircraft's composite fuselage enables a lower cabin altitude (6,000ft versus 8,000ft) to reduce passenger/crew fatigue. There are large overhead luggage bins and the highest ceiling in a widebody airliner. It has the latest air conditioning and cabin temperature management systems and HEPA (High Efficiency Particulate Arrestor) air filters. Cabin air is fully renewed every two to three minutes.

Airspace is standard but of course individual operators customise their own interiors. Virgin Atlantic Airways received its first A350-900 in 2022 and now has 12 in service. The carrier introduced an inflight bar and lounge

ABOVE • *One of the A350-1000 test aircraft on a demonstration tour in Asia.* S RAMADIER/AIRBUS

Airbus A350 operators

Aeroflot, Air Caraïbes, Air China, Air France, Air India, Air Mauritius, Asiana Airlines, Avolon, Azul, Bank of Utah, British Airways, Cathay Pacific Airways, China Airlines, China Eastern Airlines, China Southern Airlines, Delta Air Lines, Emirates, Ethiopian Airlines, Etihad Airways, Fiji Airways, Finnair, FPG Group, French Bee, Iberia, Iberojet, ITA Airways, Japan Airlines, K5-Aviation, Lufthansa, Luftwaffe, Malaysia Airlines, Philippine Airlines, Qantas Airways (on order), Qatar Airways, SAS Scandinavian Airlines, Sichuan Airlines, Singapore Airlines, STARLUX Airlines, Thai Airways International, Turkish Airlines, Vietnam Airlines, Virgin Atlantic Airways, Wilmington Trust Company, World2Fly.

Data: Airbus. Figures correct to May 2025. N.B. not inclusive of future operators.

Airbus technical documents as of May 2025 listed no fewer than 25 different weight variants (WVs) for the A350-900 and 14 WVs for the A350-1000. Significant among these is WV013 for a specialised subvariant called the A350-900ULR (Ultra Long Range) launched by Airbus in 2018.

A higher-capacity fuel system enables this variant to carry 165,000 litres of fuel compared to the 141,000 litres on the baseline variant. This, together with aerodynamic efficiencies from slightly reshaped winglets to reduce drag and airframe weight savings, enable the A350-900ULR to fly 9,700nm

nonstop compared to the standard jet's 8,300nm. Operators can reconfigure A350-900ULRs to the standard long-haul A350 specification should they require it.

Singapore Airlines has introduced seven A350-900ULRs to serve ultra-long-haul routes. Airbus is currently working on an A350-1000ULR subvariant which Qantas Airways and Philippine Airlines have both ordered (see p.36).

'Aircraft of choice'

Other A350 developments involve the freighter derivative (see p.46). Separately, Airbus engineers have worked on modifying cabin sidewalls and repositioning cabin monuments to install 30 more seats in the A350-1000. Other evolutionary changes including minor airframe structural mods for incremental weight savings, software updates, systems improvements are all possible in the future.

Airbus studied a concept for a stretched A350-1000 provisionally dubbed the 'A350-2000' in the 2010s. This was put on the back-burner but a new generation of turbofan engines opens the potential for another variant, or even an A350neo (new engine option) in the longer term.

Airbus' widebody programme senior vice-president Florent Massou told a pre-Paris Air Show 2023 briefing that Airbus believes the A350-1000 "is the right size" for the market at the moment.

FlightGlobal quoted him saying: "This is where we see the market in the next few years. I think the A350-1000 is very capable to take over from the A380s and 777-300ERs and be the aircraft of choice for a lot of our customers."

BELOW • *Air Caraïbes and French Bee A350-1000s at Toulouse prior to delivery.* P PIGEYRE/AIRBUS

Ultra long-haul

Going the distance using the latest airliners, including Qantas Airways' plans to fly direct from Australia to Europe and North America.

From early 2027 Qantas Airways plans to operate the first direct commercial flights from Melbourne and Sydney to London/Heathrow and New York/JFK.

The Australian carrier will use new Airbus A350-1000s to fly the more than 10,000 miles distance between Australia and Europe in a flight time of around 20 hours (it's the same distance and travel time from Australia to North America). They will be the longest nonstop commercial flights ever in both distance and duration.

Cutting travel time between Australia to Europe and North America by around three hours compared to the one-stop services to Australia's east coast in operation today, the new Qantas flights will show just how commercial aviation can shrink the world. It is a far cry from air travel's early days when piston-engine airliners typically took six days to fly from Australia to Europe.

UK to Australia

The forthcoming 'nonstops' from the 'Land Down Under' stem from Project Sunrise, an initiative by Qantas studying ultra-long-range flights linking the northern and southern hemispheres. The name 'Sunrise' refers to the weekly 'Double Sunrise' flights the airline operated during World War Two between Perth and Ceylon (now Sri Lanka).

Qantas introduced the first regular nonstop commercial air services between Australia and the UK in 2018 by linking Perth in Western Australia with Heathrow (QF9 outbound from Perth and QF10 inbound). Boeing 787-9 Dreamliners are used for these flights, which resumed in May 2022 after a two-year hiatus due to COVID-19.

A February 2020 Royal Aeronautical Society lecture by Linus Benjamin Bauer, a senior consultant at PROLOGIS and visiting lecturer in Air Transport Management at City University of London, explained more about the characteristics of the travel market between Perth and London.

Citing figures from the International Air Transport Association, Bauer said 41% of passengers between the two cities in April-September 2018 flying by Etihad Airways, Emirates and Qatar Airways transferred to a connecting flight in the Gulf at these airlines' respective hubs Abu Dhabi, Dubai, and Doha.

Another 26% of London-Perth passengers flew by Thai Airways International, Malaysia Airlines, Cathay Pacific, or Singapore Airlines, who transited via Bangkok, Kuala Lumpur, Hong Kong, and Singapore, respectively.

Bauer said Qantas "immediately captured a significant market share" of flights between Perth and London. There were 178,560 passengers on QF9/QF10 between April–September 2018, he reported, which he said equated to 24% of the market. Bauer noted other carriers cut frequencies as a result.

Marathon flights

Historically, the ultra-long-haul flights to have captured mainstream media attention were one-offs by an airline or aircraft manufacturer for promotional purposes. They had minimal passengers

and payload aboard to reduce weight and maximise range.

Examples include Qantas' first Boeing 747-400 handover in 1989, Airbus flying an A340 test aircraft non-stop from Paris to Auckland in New Zealand in 1993 and a Boeing test 777-200LR flying east from Hong Kong to London Heathrow in 2005 (the 'long way round' Earth on the route, as opposed to the usual westward routing).

The arrival of more efficient twin-jet widebody airliners meant ultra long-haul moved from a headline-grabbing novelty to a realistic commercial proposition. Numerous ultra-long-haul nonstops have been introduced (see table).

All these services nevertheless push the latest twin-jets to the edge of their payload/range performance. Boeing lists the 787-9's range as 7,565 nautical miles in its aircraft characteristics document, for example. Airlines eke out slightly more range by only carrying a certain number of passengers and cargo, which is how Qantas, United Airlines and Air New Zealand are able to use the 787-9 for ultra-long-range

BELOW • *Qantas Boeing 787-9 VH-ZNI (c/n 66073) arrives in Sydney at the end of the first Project Sunrise research flight in 2019.* JAMES D MORGAN/ QANTAS AIRWAYS

AIRBUS A350-1000

We're redefining long haul travel with the introduction of the Airbus A350-1000 to our international fleet with a focus on space and comfort, and designer details throughout.

Find out more at qantas.com

A NEW STANDARD IN PREMIUM TRAVEL

The A350 has 6 spacious First suites, complete with a privacy door, separate bed and lounge chair, individual wardrobe for each passenger and a 32" inflight entertainment screen.

BUSINESS SUITES

Our 52 Business suites, all with direct aisle access, are designed to redefine long haul business travel.

MORE COMFORT

Experience a new standard of comfort with 40 Premium Economy seats at 40" pitch and 140 Economy seats at 33" pitch.

ABOVE • Qantas A350-1000s flying Project Sunrise routes will carry 238 passengers.
QANTAS AIRWAYS

BELOW LEFT • Concept design for the Qantas A350 Wellbeing Zone.
QANTAS AIRWAYS

BELOW RIGHT • There will be six first-class suites on Qantas A350-1000s.
QANTAS AIRWAYS

missions. Qantas ordered four more 787-9s in August 2023.

Airbus developed the A350-900 Ultra Long Range (ULR), a specialised A350-900 model with increased fuel capacity, to enhance carriers' ability to reach far-flung destinations. Singapore Airlines was the first to introduce the variant. Its seven examples fly from Singapore to the United States on some of the longest routes currently in operation.

Airbus is following up on the A350-900ULR with the A350-1000ULR, an ultra-long-range subvariant of the larger A350 model. Qantas has ordered 12 A350-1000ULRs so it can fly the Project Sunrise routes.

Philippines Airlines ordered nine A350-1000ULRs at the June 2023 Paris Air Show, the airline's president and chief operating officer Captain Stanley K Ng saying the A350-1000ULR will "give PAL the power to match capacity closely to predicted demand on both the very longest routes to the North American East Coast but also on our prime trunk routes to the West Coast and potentially to Europe."

Business case

Connecting the continents via ultra-long-haul flights is a highly complex undertaking with various considerations for airlines.

In 2021, John Strickland, managing director of JLS Consulting and a former network planner, told this publication's editor: "You're committing an aircraft for 40 hours or more in which time you can probably do two shorter long-haul round trips. You need premium yields to justify the opportunity cost."

Yield is the revenue airlines earn per passenger per kilometre. The higher operating costs of ultra long-haul flights mean these services are largely aimed at fliers prepared to pay the premium for direct linkages,

primarily business travellers, but also less price-sensitive leisure travellers.

Configuring ultra-long-haul aircraft with slightly fewer seats to reduce weight and maximise range has a secondary effect – fewer seats mean there is more space onboard. The calculation is the increased space will be a selling point to lure the right demographics and, in turn, generate the yield to make the services viable.

Singapore Airlines for instance has fitted only 170 seats (67 business class and 94 premium economy) into its A350-900ULRs compared to the 250-300 seats in the other A350-900s it uses elsewhere in its network. Qantas A350-1000s will have 238 seats in four classes (six suites in first class, 52 business, 40 premium economy and 140 economy). PAL said its jets will have 380 seats three-class.

In his Royal Aeronautical Society lecture, Bauer identified various commercial risks of ultra-long-haul routes for airlines. There are macroeconomic factors – oil and jet fuel price volatility and exchange rate fluctuations – and the impact of economic growth or recession on demand for premium travel.

Operational considerations include the potential establishment of no-fly zones causing the redirection of services onto longer (therefore more expensive) routings. There is the impact on aircraft payload/range performance and the related issue of scheduling limitations such as late-night/early-morning departures to avoid heat and humidity.

Further considerations, Bauer said, are regulations on crew working hours imposed by aviation safety authorities, new competition on a route (whether directly or via a hub), increased security and labour costs and airport and route charges.

ABOVE • *Qantas A350-1000s will have 52 business-class seats.* QANTAS AIRWAYS

LEFT • *Of the 238 seats on Qantas A350s, there will be 140 in economy.* QANTAS AIRWAYS

Fuel price sensitivity has been a particular issue for commercial ultra long-haul routes in the past. Singapore Airlines for instance initially started ultra-long-haul nonstops from Singapore to New York/Newark, Los Angeles, and San Francisco in 2004 with four-engine Airbus A340-500s but abandoned them in 2013. Strickland recalled: "When the financial crisis hit and fuel prices went up, they had to scrub it because they had the double whammy of rising costs and lower revenues."

LEFT • *Qantas Airways ordered more Boeing 787s in August 2023.* BOEING

Flying further

The longest-distance ultra-long-range flights as of May 2025

Route	Airline/flight code	Distance	Aircraft
New York/JFK-Singapore	Singapore Airlines SQ23	8,288nm (15,349km)	Airbus A350-900ULR
New York/Newark-Singapore	Singapore Airlines SQ21	8,285nm (15,344km)	Airbus A350-900ULR
Auckland-Doha	Qatar Airways QR921	7,848nm (14,535km)	Airbus A350-1000
Perth-London/Heathrow	Qantas Airways QF9	7,829nm (14,499km)	Boeing 787-9
Dallas/FW-Melbourne	Qantas Airways QF22	7,814nm (14,472km)	Boeing 787-9
New York/JFK-Auckland	Air New Zealand NZ1 / Qantas Airways QF4	7,671nm (14,207km)	Boeing 787-9
Auckland-Dubai	Emirates EK449	7,667nm (14,200km)	Airbus A380
Shenzen-Mexico City	China Southern Airlines	7,639nm (14,147km)	Airbus A350-900
Los Angeles-Singapore	Singapore Airlines SQ37/SQ35	7,621nm (14,114km)	Airbus A350-900ULR
San Francisco-Bengaluru	Air India AI176	7,562nm (14,004km)	Boeing 777-200LR
Houston-Sydney	United Airlines UA101	7,470nm (13,834km)	Boeing 787-9
Dallas/FW-Sydney	Qantas Airways QF8	7,454nm (13,804km)	Boeing 787-9

Note: While there are fixed straight-line ground distances between any pair of airports, exact flight paths and flight times between origin and destination points move around based on the changing position of jet streams (to best use tailwinds and reduce flight times) or airspace closures due to weather or geopolitical reasons. Great Circle navigation, the centuries-old practice of following the most geometrically optimal routing between two points, is the standard measure of route length and is used for the information here.

The A350's two fewer engines, range and operating economics made the services viable again, but it was not coincidence that SIA restored the routes, and other carriers introduced ultra-long-haul services, only at a time of lower fuel prices during the second half of the 2010s. The International Air Transport Association's Jet Fuel Price Monitor shows fuel was priced at around $55-75 per barrel from 2015/16 compared to $100/barrel earlier in the decade.

Bauer's presentation indicated the fine margins involved with ultra-long-haul. Qantas' Perth-Heathrow route generated AUS$68.8 million in revenue in its first six months of operation in 2018 against AUS$67.4 million in costs, he said.

'Wellbeing Zone'

Aside from the business aspects of ultra-long-haul, there is another fundamental question – are travellers actually prepared to spend 20 hours cooped up aboard a single aircraft?

In June 2023 Qantas provided more details about the cabin it is developing for its A350-1000s. The aircraft will have a 'Wellbeing Zone' located between premium economy and economy classes to allow space for passengers to stretch and move. The zone will feature sculpted wall panels and integrated stretch handles, a guided on-screen exercise programme, a hydration station, and refreshments.

The design of the Wellbeing Zone was influenced directly by research undertaken by Qantas and the University of Sydney's Charles Perkins Centre during three 20-hour flights from New York/JFK and Heathrow to Sydney in 2019 by the airline's 787-9s. During these flights, data was collected about passengers' responses to a specially-designed menu, lighting, sleep, and movement sequences.

Cabin lighting schedules were tailored to adapt to the destination time zone. Passengers undertook simple stretch and movement activities. The timing of meal services was adjusted to align the body clock and specific menu items were served at certain times: fish and chicken paired with fast-acting carbohydrates to encourage movement and comfort foods like soups and milk-based desserts to encourage sleep.

Qantas said: "Initial findings indicate that, compared to customers on a traditional inflight sequence of eating and sleeping, those on the tailored schedule experienced less severe jet lag, better sleep quality inflight and better cognitive performance in the two days after flight."

Niche

Dr Robert Mayer, senior lecturer in Air Transport Management at Cranfield University, provided this publication's editor with some thoughts about the ultra-long-haul trend.

Dr Mayer said: "Following the pandemic, ultra-long-haul has gained momentum again. I believe we will see more of these services in the coming years, but nevertheless they will be fairly niche.

"There are only some routes that lend themselves to ultra-long-haul. At least for the foreseeable future these services will be more premium than the 'traditional' connecting services. Also, in long-haul markets generally, we have seen issues around aircraft availability.

"The lack of widebody capacity at the moment will also affect the ultra-long-haul market, which again means that supply on these routes might be supressed in the coming years and would make the ultra-long-haul services scarce and therefore even more premium."

Dr Mayer said: "There are also quite some uncertainties in the market when looking ahead. While air travel is quite buoyant at the moment, it can change quickly given the geopolitical developments as well as dangers of an overall slowdown of the economy. These developments might particularly affect long-haul travel."

RIGHT • *Qantas will use new Airbus A350-1000ULRs for the Project Sunrise flights.*
AIRBUS

777

The Boeing 777 became the most popular medium to long-haul airliner during the 2000s – and new versions are on the way.

The first-generation Boeing 777s developed in the 1990s comprising the baseline 777-200, 777-200ER (Extended Range) and 777-300, known collectively as the 777 Classics, set new standards for twin-engine efficiencies in medium-to-long-haul airline operations.

During the early 21st century Boeing expanded the Triple Seven's capabilities with a second generation of three new models, the 777-200LR (Long Range), 777-300ER (Extended Range) and 777 Freighter. Boeing's board gave the go-ahead for the 777-200LR and 777-300ER on February 29, 2000, and the 777 Freighter (a 777-200LR cargo derivative) on May 24, 2005.

The 777-300ER first flew on February 24, 2003, and entered service with Air France on April 29, 2004. Flight-testing of the 777-200LR began on February 15, 2005, and Pakistan International Airlines introduced it on February 26, 2006. The 777F first flew on July 14, 2008, and entered service with Air France Cargo on February 19, 2009.

The 777 is the most successful widebody airliner ever made. There were 2,150 orders for the aircraft by September 2023, of which 1,716 had been delivered. And the Triple Seven's evolution continues with the third-generation 777X in development right now.

'Big twin'

The 777-300ER is derived from the 777-300 (itself a stretch of the 777-200/-200ER). Two extra fuselage-body sections make the variant more than 30ft longer than the 777-200/-200ER, providing space for additional seats and more revenue cargo.

Boeing introduced a strengthened fuselage, wing, empennage and nose gear, and a new main landing gear wheels, tyres, and brakes for the variant. The wing has 'raked' wingtips to improve the effective aspect ratio and aerodynamic efficiency.

Engines are a crucial difference from the 777 Classics. The first-generation Triple Sevens are powered either by Pratt & Whitney PW4000, Rolls-Royce Trent 800 or General Electric

GE90 turbofans which develop 77,200lb-98,000lb of thrust.

By contrast, the 777-300ER is powered exclusively by the GE90-115B which generates 115,300lb. The 777's struts and nacelles were modified to accommodate the significantly higher-thrust GE90-115B.

The powerplant was dubbed the 'big twin' by analysts and media, a term subsequently used for the 777-300ER itself and sometimes even as shorthand for all large twin-jet airliners powered by efficient turbofan engines.

Other technical differences between the 777-300ER and earlier Triple Sevens included features brought in to account for the variant's longer fuselage length and the subsequent risk of inadvertently scraping the tail on the runway.

A flight software function commands elevator movements if the aircraft's attitude exceeds pre-set limits, and 'semi-levered' landing gear shifts the centre of rotation rearwards from the main landing gear axle to the aft axle.

Boeing engineers realised certain 777-300ER features could be retrofitted to the 777 Classics. A Performance Improvement

ABOVE • *An Emirates Boeing 777-300ER taxiing at Manchester Airport; Boeing has sold more than 800 examples of this variant.* MARTIN NEEDHAM

Boeing 777X orders

Air India	10
All Nippon Airways	20
British Airways	18
Cathay Pacific Airways	21
China Airlines	10
Ethiopian Airlines	8
Emirates	205
Etihad Airways	25
Lufthansa	27
Qatar Airways	84
Silk Way West	2
Singapore Airlines	31
Unidentified	20

Source: Boeing, correct to May 2025.
N.B. listing does not include 777-8
Freighter orders.

ABOVE • *Singapore Airlines had 26 777-300ERs in service as of mid-2023.* SINGAPORE AIRLINES

Package introduced for the older variants in late 2008 brought a modified ram air inlet door, software changes to improve efficiency and aerodynamic loading on the outboard wing and smaller 737-type vortex generators to reduce drag.

Workhorse

The 777-300ER seats 365 passengers three-class and carries 44 LD-3 containers as revenue cargo 'underfloor'. This capacity, combined with the aircraft's twin-engine efficiencies and 7,370 nautical miles range and lower maintenance costs, was a gamechanger for airlines.

According to information Boeing published in 2009, the 777-300ER offers 18-20% lower seat/mile costs and 21-22% lower fuel burn per seat than the (subsequently discontinued) A340-500 and A340-600.

The 777-300ER sold like the proverbial hot cakes. The model has become a key player in airline operations worldwide over the last 20 years. With 837 orders by September 2023, the variant accounts for 40% of all Triple Sevens sold.

John Strickland, managing director of JLS Consulting, told this publication's editor the 777-300ER "in many ways inherits the crown" of the 747 as a high-payload, long-haul aircraft. It is, he said, "the workhorse of airlines."

Strickland reflected: "It provides much greater efficiency than any four-engine aircraft. The A380, while a younger aircraft than the 747 with the exception of the 747-8, always had the weakness of being limited in cargo. The shape of the aircraft's structure meant the space that could have been left for cargo was consumed by baggage."

Strickland pointed out: "The 777-300ER doesn't have that challenge, it can carry large passenger numbers and their bags and still have significant space for cargo. It has the range to do some incredible missions. We've seen the likes of Emirates and Qatar Airways do 17-hour flights to South Australia and the west coast of the US. It can perform equally as well on shorter long-haul flights as well. It's a flexible aircraft that can cover pretty well all markets."

777-200LR Worldliner

Developed alongside the 777-300ER, the 777-200LR was designed to provide airlines with a capability to fly ultra-long-range intercontinental routes. Boeing says the variant can connect almost any two airports in the world; the company nicknamed it the 'Worldliner'.

On November 9/10, 2005, a 777-200LR set a new world record for distance travelled non-stop by a commercial jetliner, recognised by the Fédération Aéronautique Internationale and Guinness World Records. The aircraft covered 11,664 nautical miles on an eastbound route from Hong Kong to London/Heathrow in 22 hours and 42 minutes.

As with the 777-300ER, the 777-200LR has extended raked wingtips.

The model has redesigned main landing gear and additional structural strengthening to give it a 766,000lb maximum take-off weight. Three optional auxiliary fuel tanks can be carried in the rear cargo hold.

According to its orders and deliveries data, Boeing has delivered 61 777-200LRs to airlines including Air Canada, Air India, Emirates, PIA, and Qatar Airways. Delta Air Lines was another operator, although it phased out its examples in 2020.

777 Freighter

Boeing used the 777-200LR as the basis for a production freighter, its combination of twin-engine efficiency, range, strengthened fuselage and higher MTOW making it suitable for cargo airlines' requirements to carry lots of payload over longer distances and the need to replace ageing large freighters.

The 777F has a 226,700lb maximum revenue payload and can carry 27 standard 10ft pallets on the main deck and ten more underfloor, where there is also 600 cu ft for bulk cargo.

Boeing made various changes to the 777-200LR to develop the 777F. These included introducing monolithic aluminium floor beams, a rigid cargo barrier, a lightweight cargo handling system and a strengthened fuselage (especially around the location of the main-deck cargo door),

Flight control system software was optimised to reduce aerodynamic loads on the outboard portion of the wing during non-normal flight conditions to enable efficient operations without compromising payload.

Boeing had sold 362 777Fs by May 2025. Operators include AeroLogic, Air China Cargo, Air France Cargo, China Cargo Airlines, China Southern Airlines, DHL, Emirates, FedEx Express, Korean Air Cargo, Lufthansa Cargo, Polar Air Cargo, Qatar Airways Cargo, and Turkish Airlines.

ABOVE • *A British Airways 777-300ER at London/Heathrow; the airline has 16 examples in its fleet and uses them on routes to North America and Asia.* BRITISH AIRWAYS

BELOW • *Qatar Airways painted two 777s with special markings to highlight the country hosting the 2022 FIFA World Cup.* QATAR AIRWAYS

ABOVE • *Boeing used the 777-200LR as the basis for the 777F production freighter which entered service in 2009.* BOEING

Boeing 777-300ER basic characteristics

Wingspan	212ft 7in (64.8m)
Length	242ft 4in (73.8m)
Height	60ft 8in (18.4m)
Maximum take-off weight	775,000lb (351,534kg)
Maximum fuel capacity	47,890 US gal (181,283 litres)
Usable cargo volume	7,120cu ft (201.6m³)
Cargo capacity	44 LD-3 containers/8 pallets
Seats	365 three-class, 396 two-class
Cruise speed	Mach 0.85
Maximum range	7,370nm (13,649km)
Engines	2x General Electric GE90-115BLs with 115,300lbf (513kN) thrust

Source: Boeing, correct to May 2025.

The 777X

In November 2013 Boeing announced the 777X programme to develop two new Triple Seven variants, the 777-9 and 777-8.

The 777-9 will be the first twin-engine airliner to carry more than 400 passengers (only the quad-jet 747 and A380 have done this). Four more fuselage frames than the 777-300ER means the 777-9 is 251ft 9in in length, enabling it to carry 426 passengers. The 777-9's greater length also increases lower-deck revenue cargo: 48 LD-3s compared to 44 on the 777-300ER.

At 232ft 9in in length the second new 777X variant, the 777-8, will be shorter than the 777-9 so it will have fewer seats (395 passengers two-class) and carry less cargo (40 LD-3s), but it will be able to fly slightly further, with up to 8,730nm range.

As with previous Triple Sevens the new variants are complementary: the 777-9 gives airlines capacity (like the 777-300ER) and the 777-8 gives range (as per the 777-200LR).

Boeing claims the 777X will be 20% more fuel efficient per seat than the 777-300ER and that compared to the Airbus A350, its competitor at the top end of the passenger airliner market, the aircraft will be 12% more fuel efficient per seat, 10% cheaper to operate and generate 12% less carbon dioxide emissions.

Instrumental in the efficiency will be the aircraft's General Electric GE9X turbofan engines – the largest commercial aero engine ever developed for a production airliner, with a 134in fan diameter generating 110,000lbf.

Folding wingtips

Boeing wanted a wide wingspan for the 777X in keeping with the company's broad approach on widebody aircraft design to maximise aspect ratio. Wide wingspans impose limitations, however.

International Civil Aviation Organization (ICAO) regulations governing safety separations between aircraft and ground objects at airports for taxiway and gate compatibility classify aircraft into different design codes.

Aircraft with wingspans greater than 52m but less than 65m are classified in Code E and those with between 65m-80m wingspans, including the 747-8 and A380, are in a separate category, Code F.

The 777X's full 235ft 5in wingspan would put the aircraft into Code F rather than Code E, where the current-production models sit. The new variants would therefore be precluded from using the same gates as 777s currently in service and airports would potentially be required to make infrastructure changes to accept 777Xs.

Boeing's solution was to introduce a key visual difference between the 777X and earlier Triple Sevens – folding wingtips.

On the ground, these 7ft-long outboard sections will be in an upright position, giving the 777X the same 212ft 9in wingspan as the current models. Using a dedicated control panel on the flight deck, a 777X crew will unfold the tips during taxi prior to departure to

BELOW • *The Boeing 777-300ER has become a workhorse for airlines worldwide over the last 20 years.* KLM ROYAL DUTCH AIRLINES

extend the wings to their full span for flight, and then retract the tips after landing.

The idea is to achieve an optimum span to give the highest efficiency for flight while maintaining the Triple Seven's existing Code E classification. German company Liebherr Aerospace is supplying the folding wing mechanism.

The 777X's wings also extensively use carbon fibre reinforced plastic (CFRP) composites. At 105ft long, the spar is the largest single-piece composite part ever developed for an airliner. The composites for the 777X are produced at Boeing's Everett factory in a Composite Wing Center adjacent to the 777 final assembly line, and a Boeing Fabrication facility in St Louis, Missouri.

Other differences between the 777X and earlier models include completely redesigned fuselage fairings, a new wing-to-fuselage fairing, a new empennage, and a variable-camber trailing edge that adapts the wing position to assist with aerodynamic efficiency.

The 777X also has a gust suppression system. Wing-mounted accelerometers measure gusts over the wing and automatically send electronic signals to actuators that make tiny adjustments to the flight controls, deploying flaps, ailerons, and spoilers to move the loading around the wing.

Touchscreens

As with the 787 Dreamliner the 777X's cabin will have LED lighting, large windows to let in more natural light and the cabin altitude will be at similar levels. The 777X's flight deck is far more like the 787 than earlier 777s, with large-format LCD touchscreens with multifunction displays, interfaces, checklists, and dual head-up displays.

Just like the Dreamliner, the 777X flight control system includes

angle-of-bank protection and an automatic roll and yaw asymmetry compensation system. The GE Aviation Common Core System – effectively the aircraft's central nervous system hosting avionics and utilities functions – eliminates boxes and wiring that housed and supplied computing power.

Despite the differences, there will be extensive commonality with earlier Triple Sevens. Fuselage barrels are made from conventional aluminium like the current 777s rather than composites and the 777X will have similar flight control laws and avionics to the older models.

Boeing has also sought to position control switches in the same places to minimise pilot training; the intention is the 777X will have a common type rating with the 787.

Delays

When the 777X was launched late in 2013 the plan was for the initial

customer aircraft to enter service in 2019/20. Final assembly of the first flight-test 777-9 (N779XW c/n 64240) only began in 2018, however.

The aircraft rolled out at Everett in March 2019. Its first flight was planned for three months later, but an issue with the stator vane in the second stage of the GE9X high-pressure compressor discovered during reliability testing forced a redesign of the part and a delay.

N779HW finally flew on January 25, 2020. The aircraft tests avionics/systems, brakes, flutter, ice shapes, low-speed aerodynamics and stability and control. Three more 777-9 test aircraft followed. N779XX (c/n 64241 aka WH002, initial flight April 30, 2020) tests stability and control, ground effects and autoland systems. N779XY (c/n 65799 aka WH003, initial flight August 3, 2020) tests aerodynamic loads, engine performance, avionics,

ABOVE • *The 777X's folding wingtip mechanism is designed to provide an optimum span for in-flight efficiency while maintaining the Triple Seven's existing gate classification.* MARIAN LOCKHART/BOEING

LEFT • *The third Boeing 777-9 test aircraft N779XY (c/n 65799) lifts off from Everett on its August 2020 first flight.* JIM ANDERSON/ BOEING

Boeing 777X basic characteristics

	777-8	777-9
Wingspan	235ft 5in (71.75m) extended in flight, 212ft 9in (64.85m) on ground	235ft 5in (71.75m) extended in flight, 212ft 9in (64.85m) on ground
Length	232ft 9in (70.86m)	251ft 9in (76.72m)
Height	63ft 11in (19.48m)	64ft 7in (19.68m)
Maximum take-off weight	775,000lb (351,534kg)	775,000lb (351,534kg)
Maximum fuel capacity	52,136 US gal (197,360) litres	52,136 US gal (197,360) litres
Usable cargo volume	TBC	8,131 cu ft (230.2m)
Cargo capacity	40 LD-3 containers	48 LD-3 containers/14 pallets
Seats	395	426
Cruise speed	Mach 0.85	Mach 0.85
Maximum range	8,730nm (16,170km)	7,285nm (13,500km)
Engines	2x General Electric GE9X with 110,00lb (489kN) thrust	2x General Electric GE9X with 110,000lb (489kN) thrust

Source: Boeing Airplane Characteristics for Airport Planning, latest revision (February 2023).

and the auxiliary power unit. And N779XZ (c/n 65800 aka WH004, first flight September 20, 2020) tests extended-range twin-engine operations performance, noise, the environmental control system, and functionality and reliability.

In January 2021 Boeing delayed the 777-9's service entry to late 2023, reflecting what a company statement called "an updated assessment of global certification requirements, our latest assessment of COVID-19 impacts on market demand, and discussions with customers with respect to aircraft delivery timing."

A GE9X engine technical issue grounded a test 777-9 in 2022, and flight testing was suspended in 2024 after cracks were found in a component. In October 2024 Boeing said the first 777X delivery was now expected in early 2027.

The delays have frustrated customers. During the 2023 International Air Transport Association Annual General Meeting, Emirates' president Sir Tim Clark said he was "irritated" Boeing had again delayed the new twin-jet's service entry. Emirates has committed to 115 777Xs.

Despite the delays and a sluggish orders pace – at the time of writing in May 2025 Boeing had sold 521 777Xs since launching the aircraft nearly ten years earlier – the company is confident about the future.

The-then Boeing chief executive officer David Calhoun told the Bernstein Strategic Decisions Conference in June 2023: "It's all about those two engines replacing four. I believe this airplane will be just one of the most successful ever."

As the A380's sales history showed, perhaps there are only so many airlines who require an aircraft of what the 777X will provide in payload and performance, but Calhoun insisted "we have a lot of confidence" in the aircraft's prospects.

He said: "I believe that this could last as long or longer than the 747. When you get up into loads that airplane can handle and you can fill it with either cargo or passengers, it has real economic advantages for the airlines. And there's a big enough market there, in my view, stimulating a lot of demand."

RIGHT • *Premium economy aboard the Emirates 777.* EMIRATES

BELOW • *Boeing launched the 777X back in 2013 but the first customer delivery is not expected until 2025.* JESSICA REID/BOEING

THE DESTINATION FOR
AVIATION ENTHUSIASTS

Visit us today and discover all our publications

KEY Publishing

Aviation News is renowned for providing the best coverage of every branch of aviation.

and subscribe to your favourite magazine...
/collections/subscriptions

Free 2nd class P&P on BFPO orders. Overseas charges apply.

Big Freighters

New widebody freighters in the form of the A350F and 777-8F will keep the supply chains clicking between the world's cargo hubs.

In the 2010s the rivalry in the commercial aircraft market between Airbus and Boeing centred largely on these companies' re-engined short-haul passenger airliners, respectively the A320neo and 737 MAX.

Now there is a further dimension to the tussle between the aircraft-manufacturing titans – new cargo variants of their flagship long-haul twin jets, the A350 and 777.

Launches and orders

During 2021, it became increasingly clear that new freighters would be the manufacturers' next new products.

On July 28, 2021, Boeing chief executive officer David Calhoun told investors and analysts a new 777 freighter was "logical" and that he was "confident" it would be the company's next commercial programme.

The very next day, Airbus CEO Guillaume Faury told the European company's latest results call: "We think we have the products to be able to be more aggressive [in the cargo market]."

Airbus formally launched the A350F at the November 2021 Dubai Airshow and Boeing went public with the 777-8F in late January 2022. The manufacturers' current plans call for the A350F to enter service in 2027 and the 777-8F in 2028.

By May 2025, Airbus had 63 A350F orders and Boeing 59 for the 777-8F. Air Lease Corporation, CMA CGM Group, Air France-KLM, Etihad Airways and Singapore Airlines have ordered the A350F. Most 777-8F orders are from launch customer Qatar Airways, which converted 20 existing orders for the 777-9 to the freighter.

Airbus began manufacturing the first A350F parts in spring 2023 including the vertical cruciform, a massive fitting joining the outer-wing boxes to the Centre Wing Box (CWB). Airbus said the A350 CWB had to be reinforced to support heavier loads and containers that the freighter will carry.

Reasons for development

Manufacturers usually launch a production freighter variant of their passenger airliners, as the A300F, A310F, A330F, 747F, 767F, 777F, DC-10F and MD-11F all showed in previous decades.

There are however several specific reasons why the manufacturers

ABOVE • Silk Way West Airlines, based in Azerbaijan, is the only airline so far to have ordered both the 777-8F (pictured) and A350F. BOEING

BELOW • Airbus' A350F, launched in November 2021, will have 4,700nm range. AIRBUS

ABOVE • *An Airbus design competition inviting the public to design a livery for the first A350F was won by John Feehan and brothers Quinnten and Ellisten Iversen.* AIRBUS

BELOW • *Cargolux, an incumbent Boeing operator with its 747 fleet, has ordered ten 777-8Fs.* BOEING

decided in 2021/22 to develop the A350F and 777-8F. Design-engineering resources were available and booming e-commerce as a result of the COVID-19 pandemic boosted airfreight demand. WebCargo, a bookings platform airlines use to organise air cargo movements, reported a 1,000% year-on-year demand increase between 2020 and 2021.

Above all, the new freighters are on the way because of a new International Civil Aviation Organization (ICAO) standard for lower carbon dioxide emissions adopted in 2017. ICAO says: "Those in-production aircraft which by 2028 do not meet the standard will no longer be able to be produced unless their designs are sufficiently modified."

The widebody freighters Airbus and Boeing currently produce (the A330-200F, 767F and 777F) use earlier-generation engines. They will not meet the new standard so production of these aircraft will have to end – which forced the manufacturers to develop

new aircraft that comply with the new regulations.

The companies turned to their latest widebodies for the solution. Both the A350F and 777-8F will have features, engineering, and technology from their 'parent' designs – most importantly more fuel-efficient turbofan engines (Rolls-Royce Trent XWB-97s on the A350 and General Electric GE9Xs on the 777) and advanced materials including carbon-fibre composites to reduce weight to save fuel and emissions.

Sizing up

The adjoining table shows how the A350F and 777-8F compare, based on the relatively limited specifications data about the new freighters the manufacturers have released so far.

The A350F is derived from the A350-1000 and the 777-8F will have the key features of the 777X including its carbon-fibre wing – the longest single composite part ever developed

for an aircraft – and the folding wingtip mechanism to maximise span for efficiency in flight while keeping the Triple Seven's gate compatibility.

The 777-8F will be a bit larger than the A350F, with a slightly longer fuselage, taller height, and a wider wingspan. At 70.8m in length, the A350F will be slightly shorter than the passenger A350-1000, which is 73.7m long.

On revenue payload and range, Airbus says the A350F will carry up to 111,000kg over 4,700 nautical miles. Boeing's data says the 777-8F will carry 112,300kg over 4,410nm.

The A350F's main-deck cargo hold will carry 30 pallets measuring 96in x 125in, with another 12 of the same size in the lower hold. The 777X will carry 31 pallets (again 96in x 125in) on the main deck and 13 in its lower hold.

Essentially, the 777-8F will carry slightly more cargo but the A350F will be able to fly a bit further. 

LEFT • *Singapore Airlines Cargo will switch from Boeing to Airbus when it phases out its 747-400Fs for the A350F.* AIRBUS

Head-to-head

As always where their products compete, Airbus and Boeing each say their respective aircraft is superior.

Airbus calls the A350F "the longest range and most capable" large widebody freighter. It says that compared to the 747-400F, one of the older jets the new freighters are designed to replace, the A350F will have the same cargo volume and a 32-tonne lighter empty weight.

The European airframer says that compared to the current-generation 777F, the A350F will have 11% more volume, carry three to five tonnes' more payload and fly 300nm further at an equivalent payload.

In its marketing material for the 777-8F, Boeing says the aircraft is the "world's most capable twin-engine freighter for the future." The US company says the 777-8F will carry 17% more revenue payload than the current 777F, offer the "highest payload and long-range capability to open new markets," and produce a "low operating cost with high reliability."

Fresh aircraft with new-generation engines providing environmental savings obviously fit into the wider sustainability push under way across the aviation industry just now, so inevitably the new freighters' environmental credentials are part of each manufacturer's pitch.

Boeing says the 777-8F offers the "lowest CO_2 emissions". Airbus claims the A350F will burn 40% less fuel and emit 40% less CO_2 compared to the 747-400F and 20% less fuel and emissions than a current production 777F.

Decision-making

It seems the A350F and 777-8F will be closely matched, so how exactly do cargo airlines decide which aircraft is for them?

Various factors affect aircraft purchasing. Beyond an aircraft's pure capabilities, performance and operating economics, an airline must consider how an aircraft meets their specific needs.

Inevitably, requirements vary. For carriers serving the key air cargo trunk routes with consistent high demand for freight, the 777-8F's slightly higher payload may be crucial. Alternatively, there are markets (across the Pacific, for instance) where the A350F's range could be more decisive. Maximum take-off weight performance is a consideration for operators in 'hot and high' environments such as the Gulf.

Other factors in purchase decisions include the pricing the manufacturer or lessor offers, engineering/maintenance support arrangements, and ground equipment and crew training requirements. Operators must decide whether to stick with a supplier/aircraft family they already use.

Manufacturers emphasise the benefits of commonality. Boeing says the 777-8F will have the same main-deck and lower-hold cargo doors as the current 777F, enabling what it calls "seamless interlining"

LEFT • *Boeing has dominated production freighter aircraft sales for years, with more than 200 sales for the current generation 777F.* BOEING

New freighters compared

	A350F	777-8F
Length overall	70.8m (232ft 4in)	232ft 6in (70.9m)
Height overall	17.1m (56ft 1in)	64ft (19.5m)
Wingspan	68.75m (212ft 5in)	235ft 5in (71.8m) with tips extended, 212ft 8in (64.8m) on ground
Maximum take-off weight	319,000kg (703,274lb)	TBC
Cargo capacity main deck	30 pallets main deck, 12 in lower hold	31 pallets main deck, 13 in lower hold
Total cargo volume	TBC	27,056ft³ (766.1m³)
Net revenue payload	111,000kg (244,713lb)	247,500lb (112,300kg)
Range	4,700nm (8,700km)	4,410nm (8,167km)
Engines	2x Rolls-Royce Trent XWB (performance TBC)	2x General Electric GE9X (performance TBC)

Data: Airbus, Boeing.

(767Fs and 777Fs) and turned out 747-8Fs and 747-400Fs. Airbus has sold just 38 examples of its only current production widebody freighter, the A330-200F, since launching it in January 2007.

Airbus widebody cargo aircraft in service are mostly converted former passenger jets rather than purpose-built freighters from the factory. UPS Airlines had 50 A300RFs and FedEx Express 55 A300RFs in service as of May 2025, to give two examples. (Hundreds of Boeing passenger jets including 747s and 767s have similarly been converted.)

Overall, there is large potential for both manufacturers with, as Airbus' Faury put it in July 2021, "a wave of replacements" anticipated during the 2020s for older large-capacity freighters. The A350F and 777-8F will further enhance the big twins' presence, highlighting once more the decisive shift in the 21st century to efficient large twin-engine airliners.

ABOVE • Dresden-based EFW is a leading player in conversions. EFW

for operators of existing Triple Seven freighters. Airbus says there will be spares and tooling commonality with the passenger A350 model.

Commonality does not always stop airlines moving to a different supplier: in ordering A350Fs to replace 747-400Fs Singapore Airlines has switched from Boeing to Airbus. Generally, however, carriers tend to stick with what they know.

Qatar Airways, which has purchased 777-8Fs, also uses passenger 777s and A350F buyers Air France, Etihad Airways and Singapore Airlines all have passenger A350s.

'Wave of replacements'

All these and other considerations mean it is likely some airlines will favour the A350F and others the 777-8F, leading to each type seeing order victories and losses over the long term.

Boeing has long dominated the market for production freighters, having sold hundreds of its current-production models

BELOW • IAI's Big Twin Freighter conversion. IAI

A350F and 777-8F orders

	A350	777-8F
Air France-KLM	4	
Air Lease Corporation	7	
All Nippon Airways		2
Cargolux		10
Cathay Pacific Cargo	6	
CMA CGM	8	
Etihad Airways	7	
Ethiopian Airlines		5
Lufthansa Cargo		7
Martinair	4	
Qatar Airways Cargo		50 (comprising 34 firm and 16 options)
Silk Way West Airlines	2	2
Singapore Airlines	7	
Starlux Airlines	10	
Undisclosed	4	

Data correct to May 2025 .

787

From composites and aerodynamics to the electrical system, advanced avionics and the cabin, key aspects of the Boeing 787 Dreamliner.

Boeing launched the 787 Dreamliner in April 2004, promising airlines significant savings compared to earlier-generation aircraft in its size class – 20% lower fuel burn, 30% lower maintenance costs and 15% lower operating costs. Airlines rushed to order the new aircraft and the Dreamliner became the fastest-selling widebody airliner ever.

The positive headlines were later put into the shade. Repeated development delays meant the Dreamliner entered service in 2011, more than three years later than first planned. Issues with the Lithium ion (Li-ion) batteries disrupted the type's early operational career.

Nevertheless, the 787 is now firmly established in airline operations worldwide. There are three variants in use and large network airlines, leisure operators and low-cost long-haul carriers alike use the type. At the time of writing in September 2023 more than 1,700 Dreamliners had been ordered, of which 1,000 had been delivered.

Speed to efficiency

Boeing was focused on speed at the start of the 21st century when considering its next new airliner, in March 2001 unveiling the Sonic Cruiser concept featuring twin

BELOW • *The 787-10, the third Dreamliner variant launched in 2013, pictured during flight testing.* JOHN PARKER/BOEING

ABOVE • *The 787-8 was the first Dreamliner variant, undertaking its first flight in 2009 and entering service in 2011.*
MARTIN NEEDHAM

tails, a delta wing and canards. After 9/11 and the resulting industry slump, interest in future aircraft among Boeing's customer advisory groups switched to a different concept – a mid-size, twin-engine efficient airliner.

Boeing cancelled the Sonic Cruiser in December 2002 and, a month later, launched a concept 7E7 bristling with innovations (some brought over from the Sonic Cruiser) including the extensive use of composite materials. Boeing's board gave the formal authority to offer the 7E7 to airlines in December 2003. All Nippon Airways became launch customer in April 2004 with a commitment for 50 aircraft. The 7E7 was renamed the 787 in January 2005.

Three variants were offered at this stage: the baseline 787-8 seating 242 passengers three-class, the 787-3 (with 290-330 seats) and the 296-seat 787-9. Boeing's initial plan was to develop the 787-3 after the 787-8 but in the event the 787-3 was delayed and then cancelled in 2010.

The first flight test Dreamliner (N787BA c/n 40690) was presented at Boeing's Everett factory outside Seattle on July 8, 2007. An August 2007 first flight was planned before certification and initial deliveries in 2008.

In the event, N787BA only undertook its maiden flight on December 15, 2009 (four other flight-test aircraft flew in the following six months). The 787-8 received Federal Aviation Administration (FAA) and European Union Aviation Safety Agency (EASA) certification in August 2011; All Nippon Airlines put its first aircraft into service two months later.

Early years

Boeing introduced a complex global supply chain for the 787 in which risk-sharing strategic partners would supply complete sections of each Dreamliner to the final assembly line. The aim was to significantly reduce assembly costs and development times.

However, in the 787's early years, parts arriving for final assembly did not conform to specifications. New quality control procedures had to be introduced, Boeing sent engineers to partners to provide assistance, and the company bought-out one of the partners, Vought Aircraft Industries in North Charleston in South Carolina.

Lead times for manufacturing components meant parts in the supply chain needed rework to conform to the certified design, leading to post-assembly 'change incorporation' work on Dreamliners already produced.

A 2018 report by aerospace industry analysts Teal Group said: "Management placed entirely too much trust in the design, integration, and financial capabilities of its risk-sharing partners. This compounded the problems inherent in a very aggressive up-front programme schedule."

Issues with the Lithium ion (Li-ion) batteries powering the 787's electrical system emerged early in 2013 with incidents on Japan Airlines and All Nippon Airlines aircraft. An FAA airworthiness directive grounded all 787s for five months early that year.

The 787 returned to flight after Boeing developed several safety features: an insulator to electrically isolate battery cells from each other and the battery case, more heat-resistant wiring and sleeving inside the battery, a stainless-steel enclosure to isolate the battery unit, and a vent to carry battery vapours outside the aircraft.

A maturing production system, and the opening of the second final assembly site at North Charleston in 2012, saw delivery rates increase. Annual output rose from 56 Dreamliners in 2012 through 114 in 2014, 137 in 2016 and 158 in 2019.

By this time, the 787 family had expanded. The longer-range 787-9, which flew on September 17, 2013, entered service in August 2014 with All Nippon Airlines. A third variant, the higher-capacity 787-10, was launched in 2013. With 336 seats two-class, this variant was effectively a successor to the 787-3 in the Dreamliner family. The 787-10 flew on March 31, 2017, and debuted in March 2018 with Singapore Airlines.

Orders for 787s plateaued in the early 2010s as delivery dates slipped due to the various development delays affecting the programme. From a single-year sales high of 369 aircraft in 2007, the year of the 787-8's roll-out, orders slumped to just 13 jets in 2011.

Business picked up later on, with annual sales figures of 41 (in 2014), 71

ABOVE • *Air Canada will operate a fleet of 40 787s by 2024, mostly 787-9s such as this.* AIR CANADA

BELOW • *Lufthansa ordered 20 787-9s in 2019; the first example is pictured departing on its delivery flight in 2022.* LUFTHANSA

ABOVE • *A Norse Atlantic Airways 787-9 taxies at London/Gatwick Airport.* ROLLS-ROYCE

Orders/deliveries

	Orders	Deliveries
787-8	426	394
787-9	1,120	597
787-10	217	86

Data: Boeing. Correct to September 2023.

(2015), 58 (2016), 94 (2017), 109 (2018) and 82 (2019). The downturn due to the COVID-19 pandemic saw just 20 orders in 2020 and there were none at all during 2021, but demand rebounded in 2022 with 114 orders.

Composites and electrics

Advanced materials play a pivotal role in the 787. The major parts of the Dreamliner's fuselage – the forward section including the nose, mid-forward, mid-centre, the centre fuselage aft of the wings and rear-fuselage sections – are all made from carbon-fibre reinforced plastic (CFRP) composites.

Using large 'one-piece' CFRP barrels for these sections eliminates the fasteners, joints, doublers, overlaps and splices a traditional metallic fuselage requires. This reduces weight, which helps cut fuel burn, and the potential for corrosion which lessens maintenance burdens (heavy maintenance checks on the type are pushed out to 12 years).

The 787's electrical system is another significant design aspect. High-pressure bleed air diverted from engines is the traditional method of powering an airliner's key systems. The air drives generators that in turn provide the pneumatic power for the engine/auxiliary power unit (APU), wing anti-ice protection, hydraulics, and the cabin environmental control system.

On the 787 an electrical system instead supports many of the functions the bleed air traditionally performed. The 'bleedless' system enabled pneumatic components in the airframe (ducts, valves, heat shields, monitoring systems), engine and APU to be replaced, saving further weight.

Wing flex

A distinctive curve in the 787's wing is noticeable, especially when the aircraft takes off. What causes it?

A wing is a complicated set of compromises. A thin wing helps increase speed but there are trade-offs between the wing's sweepback angle, its thickness and shape. Aspect ratio is the width of the wing against its span.

Gliders have a higher aspect ratio – a wide wing relative to its thickness – because of the good lift-to-drag characteristics it provides for efficient flight. Generally, Boeing's approach on airliner wing design is to maximise span.

Lightweight carbon fibre is used extensively in the Dreamliner. As well as making the structure lighter, composites are more flexible. This, in conjunction with the high aspect ratio, causes a large degree of bending, resulting in the distinctive curve in the 787's wing.

In the quest to achieve the optimal performance, Boeing also introduced what it calls 'raked' wingtips to add greater span – and, in the company's view, maximise the effective aspect ratio. (Raked tips also equip the 747-8 and 777-300ER.)

Other notable aspects of the 787 wing are 'pivot' trailing-edge flaps to allow for smaller flap track fairings and help lift-to-drag. Tiny adjustments

BELOW • *The Rolls-Royce Trent 1000 is one of two engine options on the 787. Note the wing curve, one of the Dreamliner's most distinctive features.* NORSE ATLANTIC AIRWAYS

Boeing 787 Dreamliner operators

Aeroméxico, Air Austral, Air Canada, Air China, Air Europa, Air France, Air India, Air New Zealand, Air Premia, Air Tahiti Nui, Air Tanzania, All Nippon Airways, American Airlines, Arctic Aviation, Avianca, AZAL Azerbaijan Airlines, Bamboo Airways, Bank of Utah, Biman Bangladesh Airlines, British Airways, Brunei Government, China Eastern Airlines, China Southern Airlines, Comlux Aruba, EgyptAir, El Al Israel Airlines, Etihad Airways, EVA Air, Government of the Republic of Uzbekistan, Gulf Air, Hainan Airlines, Iraqi Airways, Japan Airlines, Jetstar Airways, Juneyao Airlines, Kalar, Kenya Airways, KLM Royal Dutch Airlines, Korean Air, LATAM, LOT Polish Airlines, Lufthansa, MIAT Mongolian Airlines, Neos, Norse Atlantic Airways, Oman Air, Presidential Flight (UAE), Qantas Airways, Qatar Airways, Republic of Tajikistan, Royal Air Maroc, Royal Brunei Airlines, Riyadh Air, Saudi Arabian Airlines, Saudi Arabian Government, Scoot, Shanghai Airlines, Singapore Airlines, SMBC Aviation Capital, Somon Air, Thai Airways International, TUI, Turkish Airlines, United Airlines, Vietnam Airlines, Virgin Atlantic Airways, Vistara, WestJet, Xiamen Airlines, ZIPAIR Tokyo.

Data: Boeing. Figures correct to September 2023. N.B. not inclusive of future operators.

to the ailerons, flaps and spoilers are made as the aircraft flies along so it can fly as efficiently as possible. The 787-9 and 787-10 also feature a technology called Hybrid Laminar Flow Control on the horizontal and vertical tailplanes for further efficiency.

Flightdeck

The 787's flight deck features 15.1in multifunction displays (MFDs), dual head-up displays (HUDs) and dual electronic flight bags (EFBs).

The two outboard MFDs show primary flight display information combined with an auxiliary display that consolidates frequently referenced information, such as the flight number, each pilot's microphone-selected radio and its frequency, and the aircraft transponder code. The lower portion of the auxiliary display shows datalink messages, controller-pilot datalink communications and digital automated terminal information.

The central MFDs can be split into independent formats or configured to provide a single large navigation map. Pilots can select other MFD formats including synoptic displays showing the state of major systems, an electronic checklist (ECL), and an electronic control display unit interface.

The ECL has all normal checklists but also has 'non-normal' situation checklists including the procedure to safely continue. Pilots can tailor how they want the central MFDs to present information; a single button push lets them move information around depending on the stage of the flight or which pilot is flying the aircraft.

A triple-redundant flight management system features several systems to aid situational awareness. Integrated approach navigation provides accurate guidance for instrumented precision approaches

and an enhanced vertical situational display provides a graphic rendering of approaching terrain and a clear picture of the FMS' calculated and most efficient vertical flight profile. A ground moving map shows a detailed picture of the aircraft's current location on the ground, individual taxiways, and gates to help pilots with taxiing at airports with complex taxiway layouts or in poor visibility.

Integrated surveillance systems provide weather radar, transponder, a traffic collision avoidance system,

and ground proximity functionality and Automatic Dependent Surveillance-Broadcast is supported.

Dual HUDs are one of the most noticeable differences between the 787's flightdeck and those of previous Boeings. The HUD projects an image onto a glass combiner mounted in front of the pilots' eyes and displays flight information so pilots can look outside to scan for traffic or fly an approach, while simultaneously viewing primary flight instruments.

The 787 has dual Class 3 touchscreen EFBs that work in conjunction with the

ABOVE • *More airlines continue to introduce the 787; Austrian Airlines became a new operator in 2024.* AUSTRIAN AIRLINES

LEFT • *Airlines continue to refresh 787 cabins: this is Etihad Airways' latest business class for its Dreamliners.* ETIHAD AIRWAYS

BELOW • *Not just flag carriers: leisure airlines such as TUI have introduced Dreamliners in the last decade.* MARTIN NEEDHAM

From the cockpit
Captain John Woolfson, Norse Atlantic Airways

Q) How would you sum up the 787 from a pilot's perspective?
"It's loved by everyone that flies it. We love the efficiency, it's ergonomic and the flight deck is spacious – that reduces fatigue on long flights. It has all the latest tech but still has that Boeing reliability we as pilots have come to trust."

Q) What are the best features of the aircraft?
"The super-efficient wing (people love to take photos of the wing on take-off and how it bends so much as it wants to be airborne), the carbon fibre structure was industry leading, the electronics like the AC system and brakes. It was ahead of its time going from engine reliance to electric systems. The lower cabin altitude makes this just a much more comfortable experience all round."

Q) What most impresses you about the aircraft's performance?
"Its efficiency compared to equivalent aircraft carrying similar passenger numbers. Accountants love it even more!"

Q) Tell us about the flightdeck's key features, such as the visibility of information on the large screens.
"The HUD (Head Up Display) is very impressive and precise. It allows for the pilot to become an integral part of the aircraft itself, immersing and gelling the pilots and aircraft into one system. The larger navigation displays allow for vastly improved situational awareness while the Vertical Situation Display gives a cross section of the flight path. There is overall greatly improved situational awareness."

Q) What systems do you find particularly useful?
"Having the ability to use terrain information and weather at the same time is a great feature. I particularly love the systems synoptic pages. It's clear and accurate information that can be accessed in a split second. The electronic checklists are also a leap in technology from what was available when this aircraft first came to the market."

Q) What value does the Onboard Performance Tool provide for you?
"The compare function when calculating vital take-off performance computations is brilliant. It removes any doubts and differences of opinions on interpolation, which is massive in terms of cost saving and efficiency. Every degree of centigrade we can correct saves thousands of dollars in wear and tear."

Q) Are there any particularly memorable experiences you have flying this aircraft so far?
"In bad weather and turbulence, the aircraft handles very well. Other than that, it's just the amazing crew I've met on trips and down route! I've been flying for 35 years and flown different Airbus, Lockheed, and Boeing types. Never have I been approached post-flight by passengers thanking me for such a wonderful experience as I have when getting off the Dreamliner. It really is a dream."

avionics to show maps, charts, manuals, and onboard maintenance functions. An Onboard Performance Tool (OPT) lets flight and maintenance crews carry out real-time calculations based on current weather and runway conditions.

Flight crews can use the OPT to calculate the take-off and landing and weight and balance information, with the system correcting for pressure variations, runway conditions and maintenance variations. Benefits include quick and precise calculations to help optimise performance, optimised payloads for current take-off conditions, reduced engine maintenance costs and reduced dispatch delay costs.

In the cabin

Perhaps the most heralded aspect of the 787 when it was launched were improvements to the on-board experience for passengers thanks to a lower cabin altitude, an onboard air filtration system and inlets drawing fresh air from the outside for air conditioning.

RIGHT • *Economy class on Air Canada 787.* AIR CANADA

Studies by Boeing and Oklahoma State University Centre for Health Sciences (OSU-CHS) into passengers' physiology aboard airliners were crucial in the cabin design. Research between October 2002 and April 2003 using the OSU-CHS barometric chamber examined oxygen saturation and motion sickness symptoms in an aircraft cabin.

According to results published in 2007 by *The New England Journal of Medicine*, more than 500 volunteers aged 21 to 75 were involved. They experienced simulated 20-hour 'flights' investigating the effects of different altitude pressures.

The results showed physical discomfort increased after spending three to nine hours at the 7,000ft and 8,000ft altitudes. Volunteers' blood oxygen levels were also lower for longer periods at 8,000ft. At 6,000ft, discomfort reduced, and 8% more oxygen was absorbed. There were no further benefits at lower altitudes, suggesting 6,000ft was an optimal cabin altitude. The findings led directly to the decision to go for a 6,000ft cabin altitude for the 787.

High pressurisation is required to achieve a low cabin altitude. In a traditional metallic structure this would induce greater structural strain. But composites have greater fatigue resistance, so the 787's largely composite fuselage made the type suitable for higher pressurisation and achieving the lower cabin altitude.

A separate study with the Denmark Technical University near Copenhagen investigated how humidity and different ventilation and air purification methods affect cabin air quality and influence symptoms such as throat and eye irritation, headaches, and dizziness. Filtration methods assessed included HEPA (High Efficiency Particulate Air) filters.

The study found a combination of increased humidity and HEPA filters improved air quality by removing the microscopic odours, irritants, and gaseous contaminants, while not generating unwanted by-products

such as ozone. The number of passengers experiencing symptoms associated with dry air reduced.

Boeing says the combination of the lower cabin altitude, the filtration system and the inlets drawing fresh air from the outside for air conditioning is "an optimal solution for passenger well-being."

The 787 has 18.5in x 11in passenger windows with a dimming system – adjustable by a button beneath the window – to regulate the intensity of light instead of traditional physical window shades.

There are large overhead baggage bins, 18in-wide seats as standard (though they are larger in premium classes) and 26.5in-wide aisles. The interior is illuminated by LEDs; flight attendants control the brightness and colour.

Other notable features designed to improve the in-flight experience are serrated chevrons on the engine nacelles and cabin wall insulation to minimise noise, and nose-mounted sensors that make tiny adjustments to the aircraft's control surfaces to cancel out the effects of turbulence during the cruise.

Individual airlines, of course, customise the cabins of their aircraft

Boeing 787 basic characteristics

	787-8	787-9	787-10
Wingspan	197ft (60m)	197ft (60m)	197ft (60m)
Length	186ft (57m)	206ft (63m)	224ft (68m)
Height	56ft (17m)	56ft (17m)	56ft (17m)
Maximum fuel capacity	33,340 US gal (126,206 litres)	33,384 US gal (126,372 litres)	33,384 US gal (126,372 litres)
Maximum take-off weight	502,500lb (227,900kg)	561,500lb (254,700kg)	560,000lb (250,000kg)
Cargo capacity	28 LD3 containers or 9 pallets	36 LD3 containers or 11 pallets	40 LD3 containers or 13 pallets
Seats	248 two-class	296 two-class	336 two-class
Cruise speed	Mach 0.85	Mach 0.85	Mach 0.85
Maximum range	7,305nm (13,530km)	7,565nm (14,010km)	6,330nm (11,730km)
Engines	2x General Electric GEnx-1Bs or Rolls-Royce Trent 1000s with 64,100lbf (280kN) thrust	2x General Electric GEnx-1Bs or Rolls-Royce Trent 1000s with 71,000lbf (320kN) thrust	2x General Electric GEnx-1Bs or Rolls-Royce Trent 1000s with 76,000lbf (340kN) thrust

Source: Boeing

ABOVE • *Boeing 787-8 N880BJ (c/n 66000) was the first Dreamliner to be delivered after the production pause ended in 2022.*
AMERICAN AIRLINES

RIGHT • *UAE and Portuguese flags fly from the cockpit on Etihad Airways' inaugural flight to Lisbon with the 787.*
ETIHAD AIRWAYS

more corrosion-resistant protective coating for the fan blades, a modified HPT fan blade design, a redesigned compressor rotor blade and a redesigned rotor blade seal. Aircraft underwent rectification work to install the fixes so operations could resume with no limits.

Separately, in 2019/20 quality-control issues were discovered on 787 airframes – specifically, microscopic gaps at some fuselage body junctions. Initially, production and delivery rates were slowed as inspections were undertaken and fixes made.

Boeing eventually had to pause 787 deliveries; they only resumed in August 2022 after the FAA approved production changes. American Airlines received the first aircraft from Boeing's North Charleston factory after the pause. (Company restructuring within Boeing means North Charleston is now the only factory producing the 787; the Everett plant is focused on other Boeing commercial aircraft.)

Boeing chief financial officer Brian West told the Boeing Q2 2023 earnings call on July 26, 2023, that engineering teams have got the verification work on the fuselage junctions "very steady" and "consistent."

In the end, Boeing handed over 73 Dreamliners in 2023. Wider industry supply chain issues meant a slightly lower number of deliveries in 2024, with 51 aircraft handed over. Currently, five 787s are produced per month. The longer-term objective remains to raise Dreamliner output to ten aircraft per month in 2026.

with their specific seating and in-flight entertainment choices. This means 787 cabins continually evolve; the UAE flag carrier Etihad Airways has one of the latest cabin upgrades. Dreamliners joining Etihad from Q3 2023 have a new business class with 32 seats (reclining to a fully lie-flat 78in-long bed) and 271 in economy. All seats have a 4K TV screen, Bluetooth headphone pairing, charging ports and storage.

Production pause

The disruption due to the 2013 Li-ion battery issue was overcome but further issues have impacted Dreamliner operations and deliveries more recently.

In 2017 technical issues involving compressor rotor blades and intermediate and high-pressure turbine (HPT) blades were identified in some Rolls-Royce Trent 1000 engines, leading to FAA and EASA Airworthiness Directives mandating shorter maintenance intervals and restrictions on the 787's extended-range twin-engine operations clearances.

Rolls-Royce implemented inspections, service management actions and flight operations guidance. The engine-maker also developed various technical fixes – a

RIGHT • *Rolls-Royce manufactures the Trent 1000 for the 787; the General Electric GEnx is the other engine option.*
ROLLS-ROYCE

A330neo

Airbus introduced refreshed versions of its most successful widebody airliner, the A330, early in the 21st century with new engines and systems improvements.

The A330 was 20 years old by the early 2010s and the manufacturer was aware it needed to maintain a credible presence in the portion of the market for 250-to-300-seat airliners, given looming demand to replace older aircraft in this size category and the arrival of the new Boeing 787 Dreamliner.

Airbus launched the A330neo (new engine option) at Farnborough International in 2014. There are two variants, the A330-900, and the A330-800. The A330-900 first flew on October 19, 2017, received European Union Aviation Safety Agency (EASA) type certification on September 26, 2018, and entered service with TAP Portugal on December 15, 2018. The A330-800's first flight was on November 6, 2018; EASA awarded 'type cert' on February 13, 2020, and the variant was delivered to Kuwait Airways on October 29, 2020.

'Perfect fit'

Perhaps the most eye-catching A330neos around are those operated by Condor. The Frankfurt-based leisure carrier had 18 A330-900s in service by May 2025.

Condor is using the A330-900s on its marquee long-haul routes to replace its ageing Boeing 767-300s. Regular destinations include Cancun in Mexico, Punta Cana and Santo Domingo in the Dominican Republic, Malé in the Maldives, and Varadero in Cuba. The carrier has also operated the A330-900 to Port Louis in Mauritius, Seattle in the USA, and Mombasa in Kenya.

Condor managing director Christian Schmitt told this publication's editor in 2022: "The new aircraft is a perfect fit for Condor as we can operate our long-haul flights to North America, the Indian Ocean, or the Caribbean in a more efficient way to offer our guests a more sustainable long-haul product. We are continuously reviewing our network to identify new possible destinations for the future."

'Holiday feeling'

The bold stripey livery worn by Condor's A330neos (and the carrier's other aircraft) has divided opinion since its April 2022 unveiling. Online reactions when it was unveiled were split between criticism and those who believe the design marks a refreshing change from the relatively

BELOW • German carrier Condor's holiday-inspired livery is one of the most distinctive colour schemes worn by any A330neo.
A DOUMENJOU/AIRBUS

Airbus A330neo operators

Air Algerie, Air Belgium, Air Greenland, Air Mauritius, Air Senegal, Aircalin-Air Caledonie International, Airhub Airlines, Azul, Cebu Pacific, Condor, Corsair, Delta Air Lines, flynas, Garuda Indonesia, Iberojet, ITA Airways, Kuwait Airways, Lion Air, Malaysia Airlines, Orbest Portugal, Saudia STARLUX Airlines, Sunclass Airlines, TAP Air Portugal, Thai AirAsia, Uganda Airlines, VietJet Air, Virgin Atlantic Airways.

Data: Airbus. data correct to May 2025. N.B. not inclusive of future operators or lessors.

BELOW • Airbus launched the A330neo programme in 2014, with A330-900 test flights starting three years later.
S RAMADIER/AIRBUS

ABOVE • *A330-900 F-HSKA c/n 1986 is operated by the French leisure carrier Corsair.* P PIGEYRE/AIRBUS

RIGHT • *Rolls-Royce Trent 7000 engines are the most noticeable difference between the A330neos and the first-generation jets.* P PIGEYRE/AIRBUS

plain 'Eurowhite' liveries many carriers introduced during the 2010s.

Commenters in one *Airliners.net* discussion, for instance, called it "absolutely hideous" and "gross" but in the very same discussion another person said: "Finally a livery that's fun, original and daring." Another said the scheme means "it is very easy to tell this is a holiday airline."

The leisure market is Condor's core business and using a striped livery in five different colours – yellow (which the airline calls 'sunshine'), blue ('sea'), green ('island'), beige ('beach') and red ('passion') – is meant to evoke a sense of getting away from it all.

The A330-900s will appear only in the green, blue, and beige versions of the scheme. The yellow and red are reserved for the Airbus A320s/A321s Condor uses for its short/medium-haul services.

Vision Alphabet, a Berlin creative agency, developed the stripe design.

Schmitt said: "The aim was to combine the traditional aspects of Condor with the holiday feeling and most possible comfort. Stripes emerged as a code for freedom, holiday, relaxation, and joy, similar to summer fashion or the many striped designs that come to people's mind when they think of holidays."

Schmitt said Vision Alphabet carried out more than 400 experiments to find an optimal design for the stripes that best suited an airliner's shape and captured the desired holiday aesthetic.

Whether you love it or hate it, the scheme certainly makes for a vivid contrast to the grey, gold, and white livery Condor's aircraft wore when the carrier was part of the Thomas Cook Group that collapsed in 2018.

The new scheme is very deliberately intended to signify the fresh start for Condor in May 2021 when Attestor Capital took 51% majority control of the carrier. Condor chief executive officer Ralf Teckentrup said in April 2022: "Condor has undergone a transformation: from a subsidiary of a vertically integrated travel group to an independent airline... We want to express this unmistakably."

Business class

The A330-900 has enabled Condor to significantly update its onboard product as well as how its aircraft look.

Airbus' official A330-900 data states the aircraft can seat from 290 to 310 passengers depending on an individual operator's preferences.

RIGHT • *Kuwait Airways operates four A330-800s including 9K-APF (c/n 1964) and 9K-APG (c/n 1969) pictured at Toulouse in 2020 ahead of delivery.* A DOUMENJOU/AIRBUS

Seat numbers are important for leisure airlines and Condor opted for its examples to have 310 seats three-class (216 in economy, 64 in premium economy and 30 in business class).

Condor's business class (laid out 1-2-1) has lie-flat seats with 80in recline and a six-way adjustable headrest, direct aisle access, a 17.5in in-seat 4K screen, a cocktail table and storage. Premium economy offers 35in pitch (2.3in more than economy), adjustable head and foot-rests and backrest support.

Schmitt said: "Both classes differ from each other but give guests enough space to feel comfortable on board. Due to the opportunity of the modular and customised interior of our A330neo, the interior is designed and adapted for the needs of our customers."

Condor worked with Safran to develop the business class seat and with Haeco for those in premium economy and economy. Each seat has USB charging points, high-speed internet access and multimedia in-flight entertainment.

The airline opted for what it calls a 'marina blue' colour scheme for the seats. In business class there is dark wood décor and leather that Condor says provides a "lounge-like atmosphere with maximum comfort."

Airbus' Airspace cabin, originally developed for the A350, is standard on the A330neo. The manufacturer says the LED ambient lighting includes up to 16.7 million colour combinations and 24 customisable lighting scenarios to simulate different times of day.

Condor has gone for "class-specific adjustable lighting" spanning 'sunrise/sunset', 'relax', 'rainbow' and what it calls 'Green Spirit'. Airspace also introduces a larger entrance area and more overhead baggage stowage bins compared to older A330s.

Generation change

In the Airbus product portfolio, the A330-900 succeeds the A330-200, and the A330-800 follows the A330-300. Rolls-Royce Trent 7000 engines – the sole engine powerplant available – are the most noticeable difference between the A330neos and the first-generation jets.

Airbus A330neo orders/ deliveries totals

	Orders	Deliveries
A330-900	372	150
A330-800	12	7

Data: Airbus. Figures correct to May 2025.

ABOVE • *Virgin Atlantic Airways' initial A330-900 G-VJAZ (c/n 2018) rolls out of the Toulouse paint shop.* P PIGEYRE/AIRBUS

The Trent 7000's 112in fan diameter is larger than the 97.5in fan diameter on the Trent 700, General Electric CF6 and Pratt & Whitney PW4000 that were the three engine choices on the first-generation aircraft. The Trent 7000s also have a different inlet, a composite nacelle, and a fully-faired pylon.

With a 64m span, the A330-800/-900's wings are wider than the first-generation models' 60.3m-wide wings. Composites are used for the Sharklet wingtips, upper fuselage belly, slats, rear pressure bulkhead and wing stringers and skins.

A 3D-optimised 'twist' and reshaped slats and flap-track fairings were introduced to create a smoother aerodynamic profile, and the engine bleed air system is electrically rather than pneumatically driven as on the first generation.

As with all its products, Airbus offers different weight variants to give operators choice over payload and range capability. The A330neo's basic maximum take-off weight when the aircraft entered service in 2018 was 242,000kg but various options are now available, from 230,000kg to 251,000kg. A 'dynamic payload' feature enables operators to switch between weight variants as payload/range requirements change flight-by-flight.

Airbus' Space-Flex rear lavatory/galley and the Smart-Lav 'optimised lavatory' arrangements, initially developed for the A320, enable operators to install additional seats, increase the area between seating rows or provide additional stowage.

The various systems upgrades introduced to the flightdeck of the

BELOW • *A330-800 OY-GKN (c/n 2020) is Air Greenland's sole jet aircraft.* A TCHAIKOVSKY/AIRBUS

LEFT • *Condor says the 'marina blue' colour scheme, dark wood, and leather in the business class of its A330neos provides a 'lounge-like atmosphere'.* CONDOR

first-generation A330 during the 2010s also feature in the A330neo. These include traffic collision avoidance system resolution advisory prevention, Honeywell and Rockwell Collins weather radars, an onboard airport navigation system, airborne traffic situational awareness using automatic dependent surveillance-broadcast, and a runway overrun prevention system.

Outlook

When Airbus launched the A330neo in 2014 the company's president and CEO at the time, Fabrice Brégier, commented that the manufacturer expected to "sell at least 1,000" examples. No timescale was given for meeting the target, but Airbus' latest orders and deliveries data shows the company has some way to go. By May 2025 it had amassed 384 orders comprising 372 A330-900s and 12 A330-800s.

In 2022 Airbus sold only 19 examples (ten to CIT Leasing, three each for Azul Brazilian Airlines and Kuwait Airways, two to Air Côte d'Ivoire and one to Delta Air Lines). There were also 84 cancellations during the year – more than for any other Airbus type – including an order for 63 from AirAsia.

The numbers have improved more recently. There were 37 orders in 2023 – with 20 aircraft ordered by the lessor Avolon – followed by 82 in 2024, including a large purchase of 30 A330-900s from Cathay Pacific Airways. At the time of writing in May 2025, there had been only ten A330-900s ordered in 2025, all from Saudia.

With the next Paris Air Show due to take place in June 2025, further sales were possible – but with the impact of wider economic and geopolitical issues on air travel demand on aircraft ordering as airlines reassess fleet plans, it remains to be seen exactly where A330neo sales go from here.

In its A330neo marketing Airbus says the aircraft offers "one aircraft in two sizes with over 99% commonality" as well as 95% commonality with the first-generation aircraft. Airbus says the A330neo variants burn 25% less fuel per seat than previous generation competitors (767-300ER and 777-200ER) and 14% less fuel per seat versus the A330-200/300.

The company claims the A330neo emits 20% less carbon dioxide emissions, generates 60% less noise and offers 5% better direct maintenance costs (compared to the A330-200/300) and offers up to a 7% lower cash operating cost per seat compared to its Boeing 787 competitor.

Airbus says the A330-800 is "best placed to replace ageing 767s and eventually the currently relatively young A330-200 fleet" and that having 1,300nm more range than an A330-200 enables nonstop Southeast Asia-Europe and transpacific Southeast Asia–US West Coast operations. Overall, Airbus calls the A330-900 "the newest, lowest seat mile cost midsize widebody."

BELOW • *The initial A330-900 during early testing.* AIRBUS

Airbus A330neo basic characteristics

	A330-800	A330-900
Wingspan	64m (210ft)	64m (210ft)
Length	58.82m (193ft)	63.66m (209ft)
Height	17.39m (57ft)	16.79m (55ft)
Maximum fuel capacity	139,090 litres (36,744 US gal)	139,090 litres (36,744 US gal)
Maximum take-off weight	251,000kg (553,360lb)	251,000kg (553,360lb)
Cargo capacity	26 LD3 containers or 8 pallets	32 LD3 containers or 11 pallets
Seats	220-260 two-class	260-300 two-class
Cruise speed	Mach 0.85	Mach 0.85
Maximum range	8,150nm (15,094km)	7,200nm (13.334km)
Engines	2x Rolls-Royce Trent 7000-72s with 72,834lbf (324kN) thrust	2x Rolls-Royce Trent 7000-72s with 72,834lbf (324kN) thrust

Sources: Airbus, European Union Aviation Safety Agency Type Certificate data sheet

A320neo

The Airbus A320neo (new engine option) variants have cemented the European airliner's place as the most successful single-aisle narrowbody airliner family ever.

Airbus launched the A320neo models in December 2010. By September 2023, the manufacturer's orders and deliveries data shows, orders had been received for 9,704 neos (of which 2,939 had been delivered). The huge orders backlog means production slots for the aircraft are sold out to the late 2020s.

The strong A321neo sales performance has been a striking aspect of the programme recently. This largest variant now accounts for well over 50% of the entire A320neo family's total orders backlog, indicating the industry's preference for larger-capacity narrowbodies.

In the first four months of 2025 alone, Airbus data shows, there were 164 orders for A321neos including a large purchase of 40 aircraft from United Airlines. In 2024, Airbus received orders for 502 A321neos, including large orders from American Airlines (85 aircraft), Cebu Pacific (65), Riyadh Air (60) and Jet2 (36).

Development

There are three main A320neo Family variants. The baseline A320neo with 150-180 seats two-class and 3,400 nautical miles range is a short-to-medium range workhorse. The

A321neo offers extra capacity and range, seating 180-224 passengers two-class and flying up to 4,000nm. The A319neo is the smallest family member seating 120-150 passengers two-class (maximum 160) and 3,700nm range. The A318 was not part of the neo programme.

Airbus says: "With one aircraft in three sizes the A320 Family allows operators to match the right aircraft size to demand covering the entire market, from low-to-high-density routes to longer-range thin routes."

There are two different engine options: the Pratt & Whitney (P&W)

PW1100G geared turbofan (GTF) and the CFM International LEAP-1A. First-generation A320s have International Aero Engines V2500 or CFM56-7B engines.

Airbus says the A320neo offers 20% lower fuel burn per seat and 50% less noise compared to the earlier aircraft. For operators there are 5% lower airframe maintenance costs and 14% lower cash operating costs per seat.

The A320neo with PW1127G engines (designated the A320-271N) first flew on September 25, 2014 and with LEAP-1A26s (the A320-251N) in May 2015. The A320-271N received US

ABOVE • A320neo G-UZHY (c/n 8920) was EasyJet's 350th A320 when delivered in 2019. H GOUSSÉ/AIRBUS

BELOW • Jet2's first A321neo G-SUNB (c/n 11379) taxiing at Manchester in spring 2023. JET2

Airbus A320neo orders/deliveries totals

	Orders	Deliveries
A319neo	57	31
A320neo	4,065	2,182
A321neo	7,006	1,701

Data: Airbus. Figures correct to May 2025.

RIGHT • JetBlue Airways' latest colour scheme on A321neo N982JB (c/n 7815); the aircraft has enabled the carrier to serve Europe.
JETBLUE AIRWAYS

Federal Aviation Administration (FAA) and European Union Aviation Safety Agency (EASA) type certification in November 2015 and entered service with Lufthansa in January 2016. The A320-251N was certified in May 2016 and delivered to Pegasus Airlines in Turkey two months later.

The A321neo with LEAP-1A32/33 engines (A321-251N) first flew in February 2016, followed a month later by the PW1133G-JM (A321-271N). Virgin America received the initial CFM-equipped jet in April 2017. All Nippon Airways put the first P&W-powered aircraft into service in September 2017.

The LEAP-1A24/26-powered A319neo (A319-151/153N) first flew on March 31, 2017, with FAA/EASA type certification following on December 21, 2018. The PW1124G1-JM-powered A319-171N flew on April 25, 2019 and received EASA certification in November 2019.

Engines and Sharklets

The neo variants' PW1100G-JM and LEAP-1A turbofans are the most notable visual difference from the first-generation aircraft. These powerplants have larger fan diameters, 81in on the P&W and 78in on the LEAP, compared to 56in of the IAE V2500s and CFM56-7Bs on their forebears.

Both the PW1100G-JM and LEAP-1A feature advanced technologies to reduce weight and improve efficiency. The PW1100G-JM was the first commercial aero engine to have Titanium-Aluminium (Ti-Al) alloys in the fan blades; the LEAP-1A also has Ti-Al parts.

Other new technologies in the CFM engine are ceramic matrix composite materials in the high-pressure turbine shroud. Carbon-fibre composites are used for the fan blades and fan case. The metal fuel nozzles are manufactured using additive manufacturing, where layers of fine metal powder are fused together to create parts.

A standard feature on the A320neo Family variants are Sharklets, the 2.4m devices designed to improve lift and reduce drag. Airbus introduced Sharklets on the first-generation A320 as an option on new-build aircraft and as a retrofit for in-service jets.

The engines and Sharklets mean the A320neo Family variants burn 20% less fuel, emit 20% less carbon dioxide and are 50% quieter than previous-generation single-aisle airliners, Airbus says.

Airbus introduced a new rear lavatory and galley arrangement called Space-Flex to convert previously unused cabin space in the rear bulkhead into revenue space as well as an accessible lavatory. A separate arrangement, Cabin-Flex, features a new optimised lavatory and modified over-wing emergency exit positions which enable airlines to use the maximum useable cabin length.

Since 2017 Airbus has offered its Airspace cabin – originally developed for the A350 and A330neo – for the A320neo to offer cabin design commonality across its range. The company says: "The A320 Family cabin features long haul seat comfort in all classes, from the comfort economy to the full-flat business class seat, providing the versatility to adapt to all airline strategies."

It adds: "Airspace provides passengers with the best travel experience, including comfortable seats like on a widebody aircraft. The A320 Family offers clean air in the cabin via HEPA (High Efficiency Particulate Arrestor) filters. The air is renewed every two to three minutes."

A key feature of Airspace on the A320neo is the overhead storage compartment, which Airbus claims is now the largest on a single-aisle aircraft. The bin is 40% bigger than the one in the first-generation A320, meaning bags can be stored vertically and enabling the carriage of five rather than four 24 x 16 x 10in-sized bags.

Airspace also has fully-customisable LED mood lighting (there are 16.4 million colour options), fully-integrated window shades, an updated lavatory, anti-bacterial coatings, an automatic aroma dispenser and sound and touchless control options. A modular in-flight entertainment platform features overhead and in-seat audio/video options and provision for in-seat power, wireless connectivity and mobile telephony.

Early disruption

Teething issues affected the A320neo's early service career. Start-up and cool-down issues with the PW1100G-JM prompted Qatar Airways to reject its first aircraft. The Gulf carrier was the intended launch operator; Lufthansa claimed that honour instead.

The engine experienced problems with the combustion chamber, fan blade and cracking of the knife-edge seal in the high-pressure compressor. The European Union Aviation Safety Agency in February 2018 issued an emergency airworthiness directive for the engine.

Some LEAP-1A engines also reportedly suffered problems with the booster performance in the compressor section, and there was a degradation issue with the ceramic matrix composite shroud.

Both engine suppliers addressed the issues, introducing changes to the manufacturing process and retrofitting fixes to the affected powerplants already in service.

The problems meant Airbus received fewer engines than expected. Dozens of engine-less examples ended up parked outside the Toulouse Final Assembly Line (FAL); there were around 100 such aircraft, colloquially known as 'gliders', at one point in 2018.

Several early operators experienced disruption from having A320neos removed from service to have the fixes applied. IndiGo and Go Air in India were among those who grounded aircraft for remedial work.

Production rates

Eventually the delays eased and output increased. Airbus' orders and deliveries data shows the company handed over 68 A320neo Family aircraft in 2016, followed by 181 in 2017, 386 in 2018 and 561 in 2019.

More deliveries create more revenue for a manufacturer so, with the A320neo Family's bulging orderbook, Airbus unsurprisingly planned ambitious production ramp-ups. It intended to hike monthly output to 63 aircraft per month by 2021 and to 67/month thereafter.

Airbus evolved its A320 final assembly facilities to prepare for the production ramp. In 2018 it introduced new autonomous technologies on the Hamburg FAL featuring two seven-axis robots able to drill almost 80% of holes on the upper fuselage and mobile tooling platforms using laser trackers to navigate autonomously on the production line.

There are now A320 Family Final Assembly Lines (FALs) in three continents, with two in Toulouse, France, four in Hamburg, Germany, two in Tianjin, China and two in Mobile, USA. Airbus inaugurated the second FAL in Toulouse in July 2023 having repurposed the former A380 assembly building; the first aircraft from there (an A321) is expected to roll out by the end of 2023.

ABOVE • *Azul's initial A320neo PR-YSK (c/n 11133) in Toulouse ahead of delivery in November 2022.* A DOUMENJOU/AIRBUS

BELOW • *The 2.4m-tall Sharklet wingtip devices are a standard feature on the A320neo Family variants.* M LINDNER/AIRBUS

Airbus A320neo Family operators

Acropolis Aviation, Aegean Airlines, Aer Lingus, AerCap, Aeroflot, AirAsia, Air Astana, Air Cairo, Air China, Air Corsica, Air Côte d'Ivoire, Air India, Air Malta, Air New Zealand, Air Seychelles, Air Travel, AirAsia, Aircalin-Caledonie International, AIX Connect, ALAFCO, Albinati Aviation, All Nippon Airways, American Airlines, Atlantic Airways, Austrian Airlines, Avianca, AVIC Leasing, AZAL Azerbaijan Airlines, Azores Airlines, Azul, Bamboo Airways, Batik Air, Bejing Capital Airlines, British Airways, Brussels Airlines, Cebu Pacific, Chengdu Airlines, China Eastern Airlines, China Express Airlines, China Southern Airlines, China West Air, Chongqing Airlines, Citlink, Colorful Guizhou Airlines, Comlux, Condor, DAE Capital, DC Aviation, Druk Air, easyJet, EgyptAir, Eurowings, FlyArystan, flynas, Frontier Airlines, Go First, Gulf Air, Hainan Airlines, Hong Kong Express, Iberia, Icelease, IndiGo, ITA Airways, Jazeera Airways, Jet2, JetSMART, Juneyao Airlines, Kuwait Airlines, LATAM, Loong Air, Lucky Air, Lufthansa, Marabu Airlines, Nordica, Peach, Pegasus, Pembroke, PLAY, Prime Aviation, Private, Qatar Airways, Qantas Airways, Qingdao Airlines, Royal Brunei Airlines, S7 Airlines, SalamAir, SAS Connect, Saudi Arabian Airlines, SaudiGulf Airlines, Scandinavian Airlines, Scoot, Senegal Government, Shenzen Airlines, Sichaun Airlines, Sky Airline, Smartavia, SMBC Aviation Capital, Spirit Airlines, Spring Airlines, SriLankan Airlines, Starflyer, SU Airlines, SW Business Aviation, Swiss, TAP Air Portugal, Thai AirAsia, Tianjin Airlines, Tigerair Taiwan, Titan Airways, TransNusa, Tunisair, Turkish Airlines, Ural Airlines, Uzbekistan Airways, Vistara, Viva Aerobus, VMO Aircraft Leasing, Volaris, Vueling, Wizz Air.

Data: Airbus. Figures correct to May 2025. N.B. not inclusive of future operators.

Airbus A320neo Family basic characteristics

	A319neo	A320neo	A321neo
Wingspan	35.80m (117ft 5in)	35.80m (117ft 5in)	35.80m (117ft 5in)
Length	33.84m (111ft)	37.57m (123ft 3in)	44.51m (146ft)
Height	11.76m (38ft 7in)	11.76m (38ft 7in)	11.76m (38ft 7in)
Maximum fuel capacity	23,740 litres (6,271 US gal)	23,740 litres (6,271 US gal)	32,943 litres (8,703 US gal) with Airbus Cabin Flex
Maximum take-off weight	75,500kg (166,449lb)	79,000kg (174,165lb)	101,000kg (222,666lb)
Seats	120-150 two-class, 160 maximum	150-180 two-class, 194 maximum	180-220 two-class, 244 maximum
Cruise speed	Mach 0.85	Mach 0.85	Mach 0.85
Maximum range	3,750nm (6.950km)	3,450nm (6.400km)	4,700nm (8,700km)
Engines	2x Pratt & Whitney PW1100Gs or 2x CFM International LEAP-1As	2x Pratt & Whitney PW1100Gs or 2x CFM International LEAP-1As	2x Pratt & Whitney PW1100Gs or 2x CFM International LEAP-1As

Sources: Airbus, European Union Aviation Safety Agency.

The effects of the COVID-19 pandemic slowed A320neo Family output: 431 jets were delivered in 2020. The widespread supply-chain disruption in the industry due to parts and labour shortages after the pandemic has led to Airbus adopting a more conservative ramp-up plan than once envisaged.

Currently the company is producing about 50 examples a month – the latest plan is to gradually increase output to 65/month by the end of 2024 and go to 75/month in 2026.

FlightGlobal quoted Airbus Chief Executive Officer Guillaume Faury saying in June 2023: "It's a complex system. Things are progressively getting better but it's by far too early to declare victory."

PW1100G

In July 2023 Pratt & Whitney announced nearly 1,200 PW1100G turbofans will need to be returned for inspection and, if necessary, repair after a durability issue was discovered on discs in the high-pressure turbine.

The engine-maker's parent company RTX disclosed in an earnings call in July 2023 that "contaminated" powdered metal had been used in the production of some engine discs from 2015 to 2020. The issue was discovered, RTX Chief Executive Officer Greg Hayes said, after reviewing data following changes to the design/production screening processes for powdered material to identify the contaminant.

Hayes said: "Let's be clear, these contaminants are microscopic… unfortunately, the original process, as we scaled up production, got away from us a little bit."

Hayes insisted P&W is "on top of" the issue and Chris Calio, RTX chief operating officer at the time, said P&W will work to rectify the issue "as quickly and efficiently as possible."

In a September 11, 2023 update RTX disclosed: "Approximately 600 to 700 engines will be removed for shop visits between 2023 and 2026."

RTX said the accelerated removals and incremental shop visits "will result in higher aircraft on ground" numbers. The company said it was "adding maintenance capacity, increasing part output and taking other action to mitigate impact." Pratt & Whitney is also analysing the impact of powder metal on other engine models within its fleet, although "other engine models currently are expected to be far less impacted." In April 2025, RTX said the company expects the number of aircraft on ground to "trend down in the back half of the year."

TOP • *The CFM International LEAP-1A-powered A320neo entered service in 2016.* H GOUSSÉ/AIRBUS

ABOVE • *The Pratt & Whitney PW1100G-JM was the first commercial aero engine to have Titanium-Aluminium alloys in the fan blades.* C BRINKMANN/AIRBUS

BELOW • *Aer Lingus A320neo EI-NSC (c/n 11579) rolls out of the Toulouse paintshop in May 2023, still wearing its F-WWII test registration.* J B ACCARIEZ/AIRBUS

A321XLR

Now undergoing flight testing, the A321XLR (Xtra Long Range) airliner will be a key aircraft in long-haul air travel in many markets.

During the 2010s there was increased focus on the 'middle of the market'. Broadly speaking, this term – widely used by analysts, media, and manufacturers – refers to an airliner with around 220 to 300 seats and 5,000 nautical miles' range. The 'middle' denotes how this capacity and range fits between the largest single-aisle narrowbodies and the smallest widebodies.

'Growing need'

Beginning around 2014/15, Boeing researched the business case for a new aircraft in this segment with its New Mid-market Airplane (NMA) studies. (The 'M' can also stand for 'Midsize'; the two terms are used interchangeably.)

Steven Udvár-Hazy, CEO of the lessor Air Lease Corporation – long an influential voice in shaping aircraft manufacturers' product decisions – was quoted by *AIN* at the 2017 International Society of Transport Aircraft Trading conference in San Diego, California as saying: "There will be a growing need for an airplane in that category."

During the 2017 Paris Air Show, *FlightGlobal* quoted Domhnal Slattery, at the time the CEO of the lessor Avolon, saying: "There's no question in our mind, and has been for a long time, that there's a very significant opportunity in terms of market size."

A Boeing presentation at the 2017 Paris Air Show about new aircraft development said a potential NMA would feature a 'fifth-generation' wing, a hybrid fuselage cross-section, a new efficient turbofan engine, carbon fibre composites and digital architecture.

Longer range

In the end, nothing happened. The 737 MAX's grounding after the October 2018 Lion Air and March 2019 Ethiopian Airlines disasters, delays to the forthcoming 777X and the 787 production issues meant Boeing's focus lay elsewhere.

Speaking during Boeing's Q4 2019 earnings call in early 2020, Boeing president and CEO David Calhoun confirmed designers were "going to start with a clean sheet of paper." Then came COVID-19 and any prospective new midsize Boeing was pushed even further into the future.

Airbus had meanwhile sought to satisfy the mid-market demand with new, longer-range A321neo variants featuring increased maximum take-off weight and fuel capacity.

First came the A321LR (Long Range) subvariant with 4,000nm range thanks to a third 2,992-litre auxiliary centre fuel tank and a higher 97,000kg maximum take-off weight. The A321LR flew on January 31, 2018, and following certification entered service with Arkia Israeli Airlines in November 2018. Aer Lingus, Air Transat, Gulf Air, TAP Portugal and SAS also introduced it.

Airbus then launched the A321XLR (Xtra Long Range) at the 2019 Paris Air Show. This subvariant seats up to 220 passengers two-class (244 single-class) and, with 4,700nm range, it is the

ABOVE • *The first A321XLR (F-WXLR c/n 11000) during its first flight on June 15, 2022.* S RAMADIER/AIRBUS

BELOW • *A321XLR number three (F-WWAB c/n 11080) taxies at Hamburg.* AIRBUS

Airbus A321XLR basic characteristics

Wingspan	35.80m (117ft 5in)
Length	44.51m (146ft)
Height	11.76m (38ft 7in)
Maximum fuel capacity	39,748 litres (10,500 US gal)
Maximum take-off weight	101,000kg (222,666lb)
Seats	180-220 two-class, 244 maximum
Cruise speed	Mach 0.85
Maximum range	4,700nm (8,700km)
Engines	2x Pratt & Whitney PW1100Gs or 2x CFM International LEAP-1As with 33,110lb (147kN)

Source: Airbus

ABOVE RIGHT • *Airbus displayed the A321XLR at the June 2023 Paris Air Show.* A DOUMENJOU/AIRBUS

longest-range single aisle narrowbody airliner ever developed.

Flight-testing the A321XLR started on June 15, 2022. Two more A321XLRs joined the test effort later in 2022 as Airbus works towards certification by the end of 2023 and delivering the first customer example in the second quarter of 2024.

Going the distance

The A321XLR was a hit from the outset and there are now more than 550 orders for the variant from 25 customers spanning major network airlines, low-cost carriers, and lessors – confirming lessors' views from a few years earlier about the demand for a new midsize airliner.

The A321XLR offers 30% lower fuel burn per seat and operating-cost improvements compared to previous-generation aircraft in the category as well as possibilities for opening new services that would have been unviable before.

Airbus says: "Airlines will be able to operate a lower-cost single-aisle aircraft on longer and less heavily travelled routes – many of which can now only be served by larger and less efficient widebody aircraft."

It adds: "This will enable operators to open new worldwide routes such as India to Europe or China to Australia, as well as further extending the family's non-stop reach on direct transatlantic flights between continental Europe and the Americas."

Airbus says the A321XLR will have sufficient range to fly city pairs such as London-Delhi, Miami-London, New York-Rome, Miami-Santiago, Hawaii-Houston, Tokyo-Sydney, Reykjavik-Dubai, and Auckland-Hawaii.

Fuel tank

The A321XLR has the same features as the baseline A321neo – new-generation, more efficient CFM International LEAP-1A or Pratt & Whitney PurePower PW1100G-

JM engines, optimised aerodynamics including Airbus' proprietary Sharklet wingtips, and the Airspace cabin.

The first A321XLR flight-test aircraft (F-WXLR c/n 11000) is powered by CFM International LEAP-1As. The second (F-WWBZ c/n 11058) has PW1100G-JMs and aircraft three (F-WWAB c/n 11080) has LEAP-1As.

Giving the A321XLR its more substantial payload/range performance involved introducing a modified inboard wing flap configuration, a strengthened centre fuselage and landing gear and, most significantly, a new rear centre tank (RCT) holding an extra 12,900 litres of fuel.

Described by the company as a "performance masterpiece," the RCT is a permanent high-capacity fuel tank – different to the two optional additional centre tanks that give the A321LR its range that are activated/deactivated as required.

The RCT is located in fuselage Sections 15 and 17 behind the main landing gear bay. Airbus says it makes "maximum volumetric use of the aircraft's lower fuselage."

Piloting production

As with all Airbus programmes, a pan-European industrial collaboration produces the A321XLR (see adjoining graphic).

Airbus intends to eventually assemble customer A321XLRs at all of its single-aisle final assembly lines (FALs) in Toulouse, Hamburg, Mobile (Alabama) and Tianjin (China), but Hamburg was chosen to manufacture the three A321XLRs being used for development and certification testing.

Airbus opened a dedicated A321XLR line at Hamburg to ensure production would not disrupt the

BELOW • *Airbus plans to deliver the first customer A321XLR in 2024.* S RAMADIER/AIRBUS

plant's three other A320neo family lines. Airbus designed the line using 3-D software, enabling engineers to validate the design digitally taking account of ergonomics, operations, and logistics beforehand.

Airbus built demonstrators for key fuselage structures, systems, equipment and the cabin at its Hamburg, St Nazaire, and Broughton facilities. Key suppliers including Premium AEROTEC, Stelia Aerospace and RUAG produced their own demonstrators including full-size physical mock-ups of entire fuselage sections. Digital models using virtual and augmented reality software were used to develop initial technical documentation for the aircraft.

Through the Stations

All Airbus commercial jets are assembled in a series of what the company calls 'Stations' to create a complete aircraft.

In the case of the first A321XLR, the journey took approximately four weeks. Major assemblies arriving from Airbus plants and supplier sites included the nose and forward fuselage from Saint Nazaire, the centre and aft fuselage from elsewhere in the Hamburg facility, the wings from Broughton, the landing gears from Safran and the vertical and horizontal tailplanes from Stade and Getafe.

At Station 42/43, the separate rear and forward fuselage sections – including the crucial rear centre tank – were joined, before the jet moved to Station 41 where floor panels, the cargo loading system, cockpit linings and electrical systems were installed.

Next came the most visually-impressive stage – the entire fuselage section was raised by overhead crane and lowered into a jig at the next stop, Station 40. There, the wing, and landing

gear assemblies were positioned right up to the fuselage with sub-millimetric precision.

Around 2,400 rivets joined the wing to the fuselage. At Station 40 the aircraft received its engine pylons before functional electrical power-on, enabling the aircraft to be pulled on its own wheels.

At Station 35 came the installation of horizontal and vertical tailplanes, the tail cone, flaps, main landing gear doors, nose radome, weather radar, air ducts, air conditioning and fuel systems, the belly fairing, auxiliary power unit and passenger and cargo doors. The hydraulic system was powered on, cabin linings and compartment panels installed, and fuel tanks sealed.

'Cold feet'

There are three instrumented A321XLR flight test aircraft are dedicated to validating the design changes related to the A321neo's type certification under which the XLR will be certified. An A321neo already flying (D-AVXB c/n 6839) in Airbus's existing flight test fleet will also join the testing.

TOP • *European effort: graphic showing who makes the different parts of the A321XLR.* AIRBUS

ABOVE • *The first two A321XLR test aircraft photographed from a drone.* F MONTET/AIRBUS

LEFT • *The A321XLR's rear centre tank holds an extra 12,900 litres of fuel to help extend range.* AIRBUS

Airbus announced in its Q1 2022 results in early May 2022 that it had delayed the A321XLR's service entry from 2023, as initially planned, to early 2024 to satisfy European Union Aviation Safety Agency (EASA) fire safety design requirements on the rear centre tank.

Back in February 2021, EASA announced in a 'special condition' consultation paper: "In order to protect the cabin occupants from an external pool fire, the lower half of the fuselage in the longitudinal location of the rear centre tank shall be resistant to fire penetration."

The paper explained: "The RCT creates a 'cold feet' effect for the passengers located above it, and insulation panels will have to be installed between the RCT and the cabin floor for comfort reasons."

EASA said Airbus had concluded that introducing such panels to comply with 'burn-through' specifications "is technically not feasible" due to lack of space. Decompression panels located on each side of the fuselage would be unprotected because they cannot be blocked by any insulation panels, and any attempt to install 'burn-through'-compliant material would "jeopardise" fire ventilation systems, the paper said.

The upshot, *Reuters* reported in May 2022, is that Airbus would have to redesign certain areas of the lower-fuselage underbelly to satisfy EASA's concerns – hence the delay to the intended service-entry date.

In July 2023, *Reuters* reported Airbus and EASA had reached agreement on a basis for certifying the modified fuel tank design, which reportedly includes a new special protective liner for the tank and other reinforcements.

The news agency cited unnamed industry sources as saying the consequence of the changes is an extra 700-800 kilograms in weight which would slightly "trim" the A321XLR's range from the 4,700nm officially listed by Airbus.

Heir to the 757

When it arrives in service the A321XLR will become a familiar part of the airline scene in enabling carriers to reach long-haul destinations. As well as range, the aircraft will also give airlines a flexible tool for managing capacity, for example in maintaining a long-haul route in times of lower demand when it would be commercially unviable to use a larger-capacity aircraft. An airline might also use the type to add seats to popular short-haul flights where more seats are needed.

In these respects, the A321XLR is an heir to the Boeing 757 as a versatile single-aisle narrowbody airliner in the midsize aircraft market segment. Tellingly, many current or former 757 operators have ordered the A321XLR. The 'big three' US carriers American Airlines, Delta Air Lines and United Airlines have all signed up. These carriers will use the new Airbus to replace 757s transcontinental flights between North American hubs and on transatlantic services.

For example, long-time 757 operator Icelandair in July 2023 placed a firm order for 13 A321XLRs for delivery from 2029. It is also planning to lease four A321LRs by summer 2025 as an interim step to the new aircraft.

Bogi Nils Bogason, Icelandair's CEO, said: "The A321XLR will allow Icelandair to seize new market opportunities. The aircraft will also enable the airline to reduce its operating costs, support its sustainability targets and at the same time offer its passengers the best in cabin comfort."

ABOVE LEFT • *Various current or former Boeing 757 operators, including Icelandair, have ordered the A321XLR.* AIRBUS

ABOVE RIGHT • *An overhead crane raises the fuselage of the first A321XLR during its assembly in Hamburg.* AIRBUS

BELOW • *Infographic of part of the A321XLR production system at Hamburg.* AIRBUS

737 MAX

The latest variants of the Boeing 737 with new engines added a fourth generation to the long running narrowbody airliner family.

More than half a century after the original 737-100 entered service in 1967, Boeing has now produced more than 10,000 737 family aircraft spanning the original versions, 737 Classics, 737NG (Next Generation) and the 21st century's addition to the lineage – the 737 MAX.

Boeing formally launched the 737 MAX programme on September 30, 2011, rival Airbus having launched its new-generation A320neo family in December 2010. Boeing had explored an all-new narrowbody in its New Small Airplane concept studies but eventually decided to re-engine the 737NG with the CFM International LEAP-1B. The 737-700, 737-800 and 737-900ER would become the 737-7, 737-8 and 737-9 respectively.

Different missions

The 737-8 would be the baseline version. With capacity for 162-178 passengers depending on layout it is designed for operators' key trunk routes. The 737-9 can carry 178-193 passengers (maximum 220) for operators wanting more capacity for popular routes. The 737-7 seats 138-153 passengers as standard (maximum 172) for network development opportunities, range, and hot and high requirements.

The decision not to include the smallest 737NG variant, the 737-600, in the MAX programme reflected a growing industry preference for larger single aisle aircraft offering higher capacity.

Underlining the trend, Boeing in 2017 launched a fourth MAX variant, the 737-10, a stretched 737-9 with 188-204 seats (maximum 230). Boeing also offers a higher-density 737-8 subvariant, the 737-8200, which as its designation implies has 200 seats as standard.

Design features

With a refreshed version of an established product, aircraft manufacturers must obviously introduce tangible differences to aircraft economics. Boeing claims in its marketing the 737 MAX family variants use 20% less fuel and emit 20% less carbon dioxide than the 737NG while offering 7% lower operating costs on average than the A320neo.

The 737 MAX's CFM International LEAP-1B turbofans are a principal change from the 737NG. The LEAP-1B has a larger fan diameter compared to the CFM56-7B (69.4in compared to 61in) so the MAX sits slightly higher on the ramp compared to the 737NG to ensure sufficient ground clearance. The new engines led to other structural changes: a blister fairing beneath the nose and local strengthening on wing spars, skins, some fuselage structures, and the landing gear.

The 737-10's greater length means the variant also features a modified wing and landing gear to allow for greater ground clearance when the aircraft rotates; it features the 'semi-levered' landing gear Boeing first developed in the early 2000s for the 777-300ER.

Another significant change from the 737NG are the Advanced Technology

RIGHT • *Water ingestion testing under way in 2016.* PAUL WEATHERMAN/BOEING

Boeing 737 MAX orders/deliveries

Orders	Deliveries
8,353 aircraft of all variants	1,784 aircraft of all variants

Source: Boeing. Figures correct to May 2025.

Winglets combining upwards-facing and downwards-facing aerofoils, rather than just an upwards-facing aerofoil on the 737NG's Blended Winglets, to increase effective wingspan and help boost efficiency.

Other changes from the 737NG include structural strengthening, for example around the landing gear, an extended tail cone housing a redesigned auxiliary power unit inlet and electrical rather than hydraulic control for certain functions such as spoilers and bleed air.

Despite the differences, there is commonality with the previous 737NG. Structurally the aircraft remains largely similar apart from those areas of local strengthening, and the Sky Interior introduced as an option on the 737NG

cabin – featuring sculpted sidewalls, LED lighting and bigger overhead stowage bins – is standard.

Milestones

Firm configuration of the 737-8 design was achieved in July 2013. Boeing began assembling the wing for the first flight test aircraft at Renton, the home of the 737, in May 2015.

The aircraft, N8701Q (c/n 42554) *Spirit of Renton* – also known as Airplane 1 – rolled-out on December 8, 2015. After engine and taxi tests its first flight occurred on January 29, 2016, from Renton, the aircraft landing back at nearby Boeing Field where the company's test-flying is based.

A further three flight test aircraft, N8702L (c/n 36989, Airplane 2), N8703J (c/n 42556, Airplane 3) and N8704Q (c/n

36988, Airplane 4), joined the flight testing and certification programme during 2016. Flight testing was run from Boeing Field, but other locations were used. El Alto International Airport in La Paz, Bolivia hosted Airplane 2 for high-altitude testing. The same aircraft went to Glasgow in Montana for water spray testing and community noise assessments and to Yuma, Arizona for high temperature evaluations. Airplane 3 went to Edwards Air Force Base, California, and Colorado Springs for autoland systems tests.

The 737-8 received US Federal Aviation Administration certification on March 8, 2017. Launch operator Batik Air in Malaysia introduced its first example, 9M-LRC (c/n 42985), in May 2017 on return flights on its Singapore-Kuala Lumpur route.

The initial 737-9, N7379E (c/n 42987) undertook its maiden flight on April 13, 2017. The variant received FAA certification on February 16, 2018, with Lion Air putting its first example into service on March 21, 2018.

Grounding

On October 29, 2018, a Lion Air Boeing 737-8 operating Flight 610 departed Soekarno-Hatta International Airport in Jakarta, Indonesia bound for Depati Amir Airport in Pangkal Pinang. Thirteen minutes into the flight, the aircraft crashed into waters northeast of Jakarta. All 189 passengers and crew were killed. On March 10, 2019, Ethiopian Airlines Flight 302 from Addis Ababa to Nairobi, Kenya crashed shortly after departure, killing all 157 aboard.

The European Union Aviation Safety Agency and the US Federal Aviation Administration (FAA) grounded the 737 MAX on March 13, 2019. Preliminary investigations into the accidents identified the 737 MAX's Manoeuvring Characteristics Augmentation System (MCAS) as a common factor.

MCAS is a flight control law designed, Boeing says, "to enhance the pitch stability of the airplane in a very specific set of unusual flight conditions so that it feels and flies like other 737s."

Using input from two nose-mounted sensors the MCAS was designed, Boeing says, "to activate in manual flight, with the airplane's flaps up, at an elevated Angle of Attack [AOA]."

Investigations into the Ethiopian and Lion Air accidents identified erroneous AOA data from a malfunctioning AOA sensor may have triggered the MCAS, which pitched down the nose of the aircraft despite crews' repeated attempts to disengage the system.

A further issue with MCAS identified by the accident investigations involved the AOA DISAGREE alert, designed to inform pilots of significant discrepancies between the information provided by the AOA sensors, warning flight crews when data from one sensor is incompatible with the other.

Updates

Boeing developed a package of updates to the aircraft's software, training, and maintenance to address the factors that contributed to the accidents. On November 18, 2020, the FAA rescinded the March 2019 grounding order and recertified the aircraft, issuing an Airworthiness Directive mandating operators to implement changes so they could again fly their 737 MAX.

Boeing says on its website: "Boeing developed an MCAS software update to provide additional layers of protection if the AOA sensors provide erroneous data. Prior to certification, the software was put through hundreds of hours of analysis, laboratory testing, verification

LEFT • *Changes from the 737NG include Advanced Technology Winglets combining upwards-facing and downwards-facing aerofoils.* MARIAN LOCKHART/BOEING

BELOW • *The initial 737-9, N7379E (c/n 42987) at Renton ahead of its maiden flight on April 13, 2017.* BOEING

in a simulator and numerous test flights, as well as validation during in-flight certification tests with Federal Aviation Administration (FAA) representatives."

The company explains: "The flight control system will now compare inputs from both AOA sensors. If the sensors disagree by 5.5 degrees or more with the flaps retracted, MCAS will not activate. An indicator on the flight deck display will alert the pilots."

Boeing continues: "If MCAS is activated in non-normal conditions, it will only provide one input for each elevated AOA event. There are no known or envisioned failure conditions where MCAS will provide multiple inputs. MCAS can never command more stabilizer input than can be counteracted by the flight crew pulling back on the column.

"The pilots will continue to always have the ability to override MCAS and manually control the airplane. These

ABOVE • *Boeing began flight-testing the 737-10 in 2021; the variant, along with the 737-7, was still awaiting certification at the time of writing in autumn 2023.*
PAUL WEATHERMAN/BOEING

updates are expected to reduce the crew's workload in non-normal flight situations and prevent erroneous data from causing MCAS activation."

Manuals and training

As well as the software updates, a Service Bulletin issued by the FAA on November 10, 2020, mandated new horizontal stabiliser trim wire routing installations.

Pilots must complete 21 or more days of instructor-led academics and simulator training to earn a Boeing 737 type rating certificate. To be certified to fly a 737 MAX pilots must either complete a 737 MAX-specific type-rating course or, if they are already certified to fly the 737NG, they must complete the NG to MAX Differences training course.

Boeing says: "Prior to the safe return to service of the 737 MAX, Boeing proposed a comprehensive training package with new training requirements that was evaluated and validated by regulators. The training included a new suite of computer-based training modules, new and updated documentation, and simulator training."

The company adds: "These instructional materials were designed to provide 737-type rated pilots with an improved understanding of 737 MAX flight control systems, reinforce their technical knowledge of associated flight deck effects and operational procedures and restore confidence in the 737 MAX."

Return of the MAX

Brazilian low-cost carrier Gol was the first airline to resume regular passenger service with the 737 MAX on December 9, 2020. American Airlines was the first US carrier to bring back the aircraft on December 29, 2020. Oher authorities worldwide progressively 'ungrounded' the aircraft in subsequent months, from EASA and Transport Canada to those in the UAE, Australia, Kenya, and India.

The issues identified in the accident investigations precipitated a bipartisan House of Representatives Committee on Transportation and Infrastructure investigation into the 737 MAX design and certification and the broader civil aircraft-certification processes.

On September 16, 2020, the House Committee issued

Boeing 737 MAX operators

9 Air, AerCap, Aerolíneas Argentinas, Aeroméxico, Air Canada, Air China, Air Lease Corporation, Akasa Air, Alaska Airlines, American Airlines, Aviation Capital Group, Avolon, BOC Aviation, business jet/VIP, Caribbean Airlines, CDB Financial Leasing, China Development Bank, China Eastern Airlines, China Southern Airlines, CIT Leasing, Comair, Copa Airlines, Enter Air, Ethiopian Airlines, Fiji Airways, flydubai, Flyr, Garuda Indonesia, GECAS, Gol, Hainan Airlines, ICBC Leasing, Icelandair, Korean Air, Lion Air, Norwegian, Qatar Airways, Royal Air Maroc, Ryanair, SCAT Airlines, Shandong Airlines, Shenzen Airlines, Singapore Airlines, Smartwings, SMBC Aviation Capital, Southwest Airlines, SpiceJet, SunExpress, Timaero Ireland, TUI Group, Turkish Airlines, United Airlines, WestJet, Xiamen Airlines.

Data: Boeing. Figures correct to September 2023. N.B. not inclusive of future operators, e.g., IAG (50 aircraft).

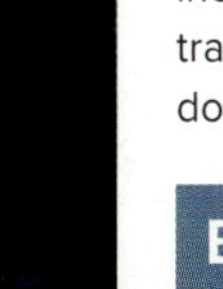

Boeing 737 MAX basic characteristics

	737-7	737-8/8200	737-9	737-10
Wingspan	117ft 10in (35.9m)	117ft 10in (35.9m)	117ft 10in (35.9m)	117ft 10in (35.9m)
Length	116ft 8in (35.56m)	129ft 8in (39.52m)	138ft 4in (42.16m)	143ft 8in (43.8m)
Height	40ft 4in (12.3m)	40ft 4in (12.3m)	40ft 4in (12.3m)	40ft 4in (12.3m)
Maximum fuel capacity	6,820 US gal (25,800 litres)	6,820 US gal (25,800 litres)	6,820 US gal (25,800 litres)	6,820 US gal (25,800 litres)
Maximum take-off weight	177,000lb (80,000kg)	182,000lb (82,600kg)	194,700lb (88,300kg)	197,900lb (89,800kg)
Seats	138-153, or 172 maximum	162-178, or 210 maximum	178-193, or 220 maximum	188-204, or 230 maximum
Cruise speed	Mach 0.79	Mach 0.79	Mach 0.79	Mach 0.79
Maximum range	3,850nm (7,130km)	3,550nm (6,570km)	3,550nm (6,570km)	3,300nm (6,100km)
Engines	2x CFM International LEAP-1Bs	2x CFM International LEAP-1Bs	2x CFM International LEAP-1Bs	2x CFM International LEAP-1Bs

Source: Boeing

its report. Its executive summary says "technical design flaws, faulty assumptions about pilot responses, and management failures by both Boeing and the Federal Aviation Administration played instrumental and causative roles" in the Lion Air and Ethiopian crashes.

The report says: "Boeing's design and development of the 737 MAX was marred by technical design failures, lack of transparency with both regulators and customers, and efforts to downplay or disregard concerns about the operation of the aircraft."

Boeing's response to the House report issued on September 16, 2020, said: "Multiple committees, experts, and governmental authorities have examined issues related to the MAX, and we have incorporated many of their recommendations, as well as the results of our own internal reviews, into the 737 MAX and the overall airplane design process."

It continued: "We have also taken steps to bolster safety across our company, consulting outside experts and learning from best practices in other industries. We have set up a new safety organization to enhance and standardize safety practices, restructured our engineering organization to give engineers a stronger voice and a more direct line to share concerns with top management, created a permanent Aerospace Safety Committee of our Board of Directors as well as expanded the role of the Safety Promotion Center."

Boeing added: "We have learned many hard lessons as a company from the accidents of Lion Air Flight 610 and Ethiopian Airlines Flight 302, and from the mistakes we have made. We have made fundamental changes to our company as a result and continue to look for ways to improve. Change

LEFT • *Southwest Airlines received its initial 737-8 in 2017; with more than 200 examples in service it flies more 737 MAX aircraft than any other airline.* ASHLEE D SMITH/ SOUTHWEST AIRLINES

BELOW • *Qatar Airways had nine 737-8s in service as of mid-2023.* QATAR AIRWAYS

ABOVE • *Ryanair has ordered 300 737-10s (150 firm, 150 options) for delivery from 2028 to 2033. It is already receiving 737-8200s.* BOEING

BELOW • *Boeing developed a package of updates to the 737 MAX's flight control software, training, and maintenance.* BOEING

is always hard and requires daily commitment, but we as a company are dedicated to doing the work."

After the House Committee report in 2020, a comprehensive bipartisan bill seeking to reform the FAA certification and regulatory processes was unveiled. The Aircraft Certification Reform and Accountability Act directs the FAA administrator to require certain safety standards during aircraft certification.

There are new requirements for disclosing safety-critical information. The bill also reinforces protection for whistle-blowers, strengthens civil penalties for regulatory violations, and directs the FAA to set global standards to enhance pilot training.

Next steps

Both the 737-7 and 737-10 variants of the 737 MAX were still awaiting certification at the time of writing in May 2025. Flight-testing of the 737-7 (using N7201S c/n 42561) began on March 16, 2018, and with the 737-10 (using N27751 c/n 66122) on June 18, 2021.

Boeing has to rework aircraft already in service or assembled with the mandated software and hardware changes. Boeing chief financial officer Brian West told the company's second-quarter 2023 results presentation on July 26, 2023, that the company had approximately 220 MAX aircraft in its inventory at the end of the quarter.

The rework activities have affected 737 MAX output, as has the wider supply-chain disruption to have impacted all commercial aircraft production after the COVID-19 pandemic. Other snags emerged during 2023 – firstly, improperly-installed brackets joining the aft fuselage to the vertical tail and, in August, improperly-drilled holes on the aft fuselage.

A further issue affecting the pace of 737 MAX output has been the impact of tighter regulatory scrutiny on production following the January 2024 incident where the door plug of an Alaska Airlines 737-9 blew out shortly after take-off from Portland, Oregon, caused by missing door plug bolts.

Boeing continues to receive 737 MAX orders. The company does not break down information by variant, but its official orders and deliveries data shows it had received 8,353 orders for all variants of the aircraft by May 2025.

Recent orders include those from American Airlines (85 aircraft), the lessors Avia Solutions Group (40) and BOC Aviation (69), and Japan Airlines (17). Pegasus Airlines in Turkey ordered 100 examples.

A220

The Airbus A220, formerly the Bombardier C Series, has become ever more familiar at airports worldwide. What features make the little twin-jet tick?

Back in the mid-2000s Bombardier Aerospace in Canada had grand designs on becoming a larger player in commercial airliner production by launching an ambitious new aircraft, the C Series, packed with new technologies. Within two decades Airbus had acquired the programme. The A220, as it is now known, is a crucial part of the European company's product line.

Origins

Bombardier launched the C Series in July 2008 with two variants: the baseline CS100 (now the A220-100) and a slightly larger and longer-range CS300 (now the A220-300).

Originally the CS100 was due to fly in 2011 and enter service in 2013, but development delays meant the first flight-test aircraft only flew on September 18, 2013. Certification followed on December 18, 2015, with Swiss International Air Lines introducing it on July 15, 2016. The A220-300 conducted its first flight on July 11, 2016, entering service with airBaltic on December 14, 2016.

The C Series became the A220 in July 2018 after Airbus acquired a 50.1% majority stake in the programme. Airbus later increased its stake to 75% as Bombardier left the programme; the remaining 25% stake is held by Investissement Québec, the investment arm of the Québec government.

By September 2023, some 283 A220s had been delivered to 16 operators, Airbus' official orders and deliveries data shows. The type is active in all the key air transport markets: Europe, North America, Asia-Pacific, the Middle East, and Africa.

According to Airbus, the type is now operated on more than 1,100 routes connecting 375 destinations. The in-service fleet has exceeded 770,000 flight cycles and well over one million flight hours. The type routinely hits more than 99% operational reliability.

Orders totalled 806 aircraft by September 2023. Even without further new business, Airbus has a backlog of more than 500 A220s to produce at its two final assembly lines for the type in Mirabel, Canada (the original C Series factory) and at the Airbus US manufacturing facility at the Brookley Aeroplex in Mobile, Alabama, where A320s and A321s are also assembled.

With an industry ever-more fixed on introducing the cleanest and most efficient aircraft, the A220's presence at airports worldwide is only likely to increase.

Trade spat

A few months after the C Series variants' service debuts, the aircraft became the subject of a trade dispute between the United States and Canada. Boeing filed a complaint with the US Department of Commerce in April 2017, claiming Delta Air Lines' order for 75 C Series placed in 2016

BELOW • *The A220-300 pictured during an early test flight.*
S RAMADIER/AIRBUS

ABOVE • *Breeze Airways began flying the A220-300 in 2022.* TAD DENSON/AIRBUS

was made possible by Canadian government subsidies enabling Bombardier to 'dump' the aircraft (that is, selling at below-cost prices).

The US Department of Commerce sided with Boeing and imposed nearly 300% import duties (an initial 219.6% levy followed a few weeks later by an additional 79.8%). Bombardier argued against the duties by saying Boeing could not have been harmed because it did not have a product like the C Series in its portfolio.

In the end, the US International Trade Commission (ITC) agreed

with Bombardier. Early in 2018 the commission ruled the C Series did not harm Boeing and overturned the Commerce Department's action.

By that time, however, the wider picture had changed. Bombardier had started to restructure its aerospace activities; it sold off the CL-415 firefighting aircraft programme in 2016 and the Dash 8 turboprop two years later.

In October 2017, after the Commerce Department announced the duties, Bombardier had struck a deal with Airbus over the sale of a 50.01% majority stake in the C Series programme.

A new C Series Aircraft Limited Partnership (CSALP) was established, in which Bombardier Inc and Investissement Québec (acting for the government of Québec) held stakes. Airbus announced a plan to produce C Series for US customers at its Mobile plant.

After the ITC ruling, Airbus took full control of the CSALP in July 2018. The C Series was rebranded as the A220 and the CSALP changed its name to Airbus Canada Limited.

Airbus in 2019 started constructing a 270,000sq ft building at Mobile containing a dedicated A220 assembly line. Delta Air Lines received the first Mobile-assembled A220 in October 2020.

Airbus buying the C Series added a fresh dimension to the competition between the two major commercial aircraft manufacturers. The European company brought an advanced new product into its portfolio and strengthened its presence at the lower end of the narrowbody airliner market.

Airbus subsequently announced the ACJTwoTwenty, a business jet variant. The first example of this 18-passenger, 5,650 nautical miles-range model conducted its first flight in December 2021.

Big savings

The A220 was designed for the 100-to-160 seats segment of the 

A220 orders/deliveries totals

	Orders	Deliveries
A220-100	98	71
A220-300	806	342

Source: Airbus. Figures correct to May 2025.

commercial aircraft market – the gap between the largest regional jets and the smallest single-aisle narrowbodies of the A320/737 size.

Around 50% of the A220's structure is made from carbon fibre composites including the wing, rear fuselage, empennage, vertical and horizontal stabilisers, elevators, flaps, spoilers, and engine nacelles. Aluminium-lithium and titanium account for more than 30%.

These materials, in conjunction with the aircraft's Pratt & Whitney PurePower PW1500G-series geared turbofan engines, advanced aerodynamics and an integrated three-axis fly-by-wire flight control system (which moves the aircraft's centre of gravity in flight to minimise drag), generate some impressive numbers.

The A220 uses 25% less fuel, emits 25% less carbon dioxide per seat, produces 50% less nitrous oxide and is 25% cheaper to operate per seat compared to previous-generation aircraft in its size category, Airbus says.

As well as these stated savings the A220 also offers impressive range – the A220-100 can fly 3,450nm and the A220-300 can do 3,400nm.

Jonathan Hayes, chief pilot of the US airline Breeze Airways which introduced the A220 in 2022, told *Aviation News*: "The range of this aircraft is absolutely ridiculous for its size. The Pratt & Whitney Geared Turbo Fan engines have an impressively low fuel burn. This aircraft has no problem at all going all the way 'transcon' from the northeast to the coastal west [in the United States]."

Replacements

Unsurprisingly many airlines have turned to the A220 to refresh their fleets.

From the cockpit

BREEZE AIRWAYS' chief pilot Jonathan Hayes told this publication's editor: "The first impression is that it is a very cool-looking airplane. It's got great lines and looks very sleek. If you ask me, you won't find a nicer office than the flight deck of an A220."

Hayes said: "Stepping onto the flight deck you are immediately struck by how modern it looks. The large display units are very crisp and clear, providing an impressive amount of information in one place. Its design is a great combination of state-of-the-art fly-by-wire with sidestick while also being a very pilot friendly airplane to fly."

He continued: "The large screens have a great presentation with map like terrain overlay. The cursor can move between four of the display unit fields and perform flight management system functions or graphical rerouting right on the map. The unique aspect of the Collins suite is the ability to accomplish the same task about four different ways based on your preferences.

Hayes said: "The greatest functionality of the A220 flight deck is the Electronic Checklist. The ECL performs all normal, abnormal, and emergency checklists and procedures and is a great task management tool."

He feels the best feature of the A220 "is the conventional feel to the sidestick coupled with traditional throttles. Having flown the A320 family for over 12,000 hours it has been a nice change." On performance, Hayes said: "The A220 has great short field performance. It can very comfortably land at some of the smaller airports we operate in/out of."

A statement from Air Baltic said: "The A220-300 offers an incredibly pilot-friendly cockpit environment. Ergonomics are thoughtfully designed, allowing smooth and intuitive interactions with aircraft controls and systems. Our pilots appreciate the array of support systems in place, empowering them to execute each flight with the utmost safety and efficiency."

Air Baltic added: "One of the most impressive features of the A220-300 are five big screens in the cockpit. These screens deliver detailed data, enabling our pilots to closely track flight progress and monitor all systems on board. Whether it is a short, 30-minute flight or a more extended journey to destinations like Dubai and Tenerife, our pilots have everything they need to ensure a safe and enjoyable flight experience."

LEFT • *Air Canada had 60 A220s on order as of mid-2023.* AIR CANADA

BELOW • *Two of Air Baltic's A220 fleet wear the flag colours of the airline's home nation, Latvia.* AIR BALTIC

At Delta Air Lines, the A220 replaced Boeing 717s and McDonnell Douglas MD-88s/MD-90s on the carrier's bread-and-butter services to major hubs from US domestic airports. Delta operates more A220s than any other airline; it had 63 in service as of September 2023 comprising 45 A220-100s and 18 A220-300s.

Delta appreciates the type to the point that it has reordered the A220 five times, most recently in July 2023 when it exercised options for 12 A220-300s that will take its total fleet to 131 A220 family aircraft.

Kristen Bojko, Delta's vice-president of fleet, said: "The A220-300 offers efficient performance and flexibility. The continuing expansion of Delta's A220 family is an integral investment in the future of sustainable aviation."

Qantas Airways is due to receive the first of 29 A220-300s by the end of 2023 (it has options on a further eight). The A220 will gradually replace QantasLink's Boeing 717 fleet on routes across Australia.

Qantas said in May 2023 that its first A220 will fly between Melbourne and Canberra, with subsequent aircraft to be deployed to other parts of the regional and domestic network.

The carrier said: "With double the range of the Boeing 717, the A220 has the ability to fly between any city in Australia, paving the way for new domestic and short-haul international routes as more aircraft join our fleet."

At Air France, A220-300s are replacing the A318 and A319 on the short/medium-haul network. The carrier's first example was delivered in September 2021, and it had received 28 by September 2023. All 60 examples Air France has ordered are due to be handed over by the end of 2025, which the airline has described as the fastest service entry of a new type in its history.

Launch operators Swiss and Air Baltic also used the A220 to refresh their fleets, respectively Avro RJs and Dash 8s.

Flexibility

The A220 is more than a leaner, greener, and cheaper-to-operate successor to older and less efficient aircraft. The type's economics and range provide new capabilities.

Airlines like having aircraft with different seat counts so they can 'right size' according to demand. Putting an optimum number of seats on a route matters, because too much capacity risks losing money and too little risks missing out on growth.

Although A320/737-sized narrowbodies or smaller widebody aircraft (for example, A330s or 767s) can operate medium-haul, these aircraft typically have too many seats to make viable routes to airports with less passenger traffic (known

ABOVE • *Pilots praise the A220's flight deck with the large-format display screens.* H GOUSSÉ/AIRBUS

BELOW • *A220s are an increasingly familiar sight at airports, as here at Manchester.* MARTIN NEEDHAM

Airbus A220 basic characteristics

	A220-100	A220-300
Wingspan	35.1m (115ft 1in)	35.1m (115ft 1in)
Length	35m (115ft)	35m (115ft)
Height	11.50m (37ft 7in)	11.50m (37ft 7in)
Maximum fuel capacity	21,918 litres (5,790 US gal)	21,918 litres (5,790 US gal)
Maximum take-off weight	63,100kg (139,000lb)	70,900kg (156,000lb)
Seats	100-120 two-class	120-150 two-class
Cruise speed	Mach 0.82	Mach 0.82
Maximum range	3,450nm (6,390km)	3,600nm (6,700km)
Engines	2x Pratt & Whitney PW1500G	2x Pratt & Whitney PW1500G

Source: Airbus

Airbus A220 operators

Air Austral, Air Baltic, Air Canada, Air France, Air Manas, Air Sénégal, Air Tanzania, Air Vanuatu, Breeze Airways, Bulgaria Air, Croatia Airlines, Delta Air Lines, Government/VIP, Ibom Air, Iraqi Airways, ITA Airways, JetBlue Airways, Korean Air, Qantas Airways, Swiss International Air Lines.

Source: Airbus, figures correct to May 2025.

Middle East, North Africa and the Caucasus."

The A220 is also intrinsic to the business model of Breeze Airways, which uses the aircraft to fly to underserved communities in the US.

As Breeze's chief pilot Jonathan Hayes said, the Salt Lake City, Utah-based carrier's A220s operate various coast-to-coast routes – and these include routes between hubs and secondary destinations that have never been operated before, including Los Angeles-Providence, San Fransisco-Raleigh, and Las Vegas-Syracuse.

Breeze's co-founder and chief executive is David Neeleman, who previously set up JetBlue Airways and Azul, among other carriers. Neeleman said in May 2023: "The A220 has been

as 'secondary' destinations in industry jargon) or those with inconsistent demand.

The A220 can help by fitting into the gap on payload/range between regional jets and larger single-aisles. If deploying an A320/737 on a route is marginal, the A220 enables an airline to continue operating the service with a more suitable seat count and therefore a better cost. Alternatively, a carrier can try out a new service with lower risk than putting a larger-capacity type onto the route.

'Transformed'

The A220 gives airlines another arrow in their network-planning bow. It also offers new route development possibilities. Air Baltic for instance, based in the Latvian capital Riga, now serves destinations such as Dubai, Marrakech, Gran Canaria, and Tenerife it was unable to reach before when it used Dash 8s.

Air Baltic told this author in 2023: "The A220-300 has transformed our airline. [It] goes hand in hand with the company's overall network management strategy. This winter season, we will fly to Tenerife in the Canary Islands from all four of our bases." The A220-300, the airline said, will enable it to "continue to develop its network in Europe, the

LEFT • *Airbus fully acquired the former C Series from Bombardier in 2018 and rebranded it as the A220.* S RAMADIER/AIRBUS

BELOW • *With 100 on order, JetBlue Airways will have more A220s than any other airline.* JETBLUE AIRWAYS

ABOVE • *Delta Air Lines' first A220-100 is rolled out at the Mirabel factory.* P DESROCHERS/AIRBUS

foundational to the growth and success of Breeze. We've been able to link new city pairs while reducing operating costs and environmental impact."

Breeze operated 39 A220-300s as of May 2025 and it is set to become a key operator of the type, having ordered 90 examples with deliveries out to 2027/28.

The carrier is on a recruitment drive. Hayes told *Aviation News*: "Breeze is looking for 40 direct entry captains for the A220 to be in class by March, so reach out on the Breeze website if you're interested."

For passengers, an A220 provides a pleasant environment with large windows, 18.5in-wide seats as standard in a five-abreast layout, large overhead stowage bins and LED mood lighting. When Delta introduced the A220 in 2018 the airline's CEO Ed Bastian said the aircraft was the "nicest domestic product in the skies."

In mid-2023, Air Baltic told this publication's editor that the carrier's passengers have "overwhelmingly positive" feedback about the comfort level aboard the A220. The carrier said: "It offers an excellent flying experience with benefits for passengers such as wider seats, larger windows, more hand luggage space and more space."

RIGHT • *Overhead storage bins in the A220 cabin.* C SANTANA/AIRBUS

BELOW • *The A220 has extended Air Baltic's geographical footprint to the Middle East and North Africa.* AIR BALTIC

Evolution

Manufacturers always like to extract the best performance from their aircraft by taking advantage of any inherent margin in the design and the A220 is no exception. In 2019 Airbus increased basic maximum take-off weight on both variants (to 63,100kg on the A220-100 and 70,000kg on the A220-300) and extended range by 450nm.

More substantial evolution is likely. A larger A220 has been on the cards since the programme's early days and Airbus chief executive officer Guillaume Faury said in January 2023 further development is a case of "when, not if."

Reports in 2023, for example in *Bloomberg*, said plans are advancing for a third variant seating around 170 passengers with both Pratt & Whitney and CFM International engine options – a contrast to the current models, where P&W is the single-source engine supplier.

Such an aircraft, Faury said in June 2023, would give Airbus a "complete family" at the lower end of its product range and be a clean-sheet successor in the company's portfolio to the 110-to-160-seat A319neo, the lowest-capacity A320neo variant.

A prospective third A220 has been dubbed the A220-500 but during the 2023 Paris Air Show, Airbus' chief commercial officer at the time, Christian Scherer told *The Air Current* the company actually refers to the variant as the A221.

Faury said in Airbus' annual results in February 2023 that achieving profitability on the current A220 models matters before decisions are made about developing the aircraft. "We have a lot on our plate," he said.

Equally, Faury acknowledged "a very strong appetite" for a larger A220, mirroring the broader shift in commercial aviation towards larger narrowbody airliners.

Turboprops

Turboprop airliners might not have jet aircraft glamour but they have significant roles – and they have developed during the 21st century.

Turboprops have a valuable role in air transport by flying people and goods between regional airports, between regions and larger hubs and to the very smallest communities in remote regions where they provide lifeline connectivity.

The ATR 42/72 and De Havilland Canada (DHC) Dash 8 Series 400 were the two main turboprop airliners in production early in the 21st century, after several manufacturers that previously produced aircraft for the segment (BAE Systems, Fairchild Dornier, Saab) left the market during the 1990s.

New generation

Bombardier Aerospace in Canada, which had acquired DHC's products and type certificates in 1992, launched a fourth-generation Dash 8 – also known as the Q400 – in June 1995. Test flights began in January 1998 but it only entered service with SAS Commuter on January 20, 2000.

ATR launched the ATR 600 Series in October 2007. The 72-600 prototype flew on July 24, 2009 and Royal Air Maroc introduced it to service in 2011. The 42-600 few on March 4, 2010 and entered service with Precision Air Services in Tanzania in 2012.

Both the Q400 and ATR 600 Series feature Pratt & Whitney Canada turboprop engines (PW150A on the Dash, P127M on the ATRs) and Thales glass cockpits.

Avionics to maximise pilots' situational awareness and assist in workload management include traffic collision and avoidance system, required navigation performance with authorisation required (RNP-AR), localiser performance with vertical guidance (LPV), vertical navigation (VNAV), automatic dependent surveillance broadcast-out and electronic flight bag compatibility.

LPV enables precision approaches (minimums of up to 200ft visibility based on GPS information without the need for support from a ground station), RNP-AR enables trajectories to be followed to within 0.1-mile accuracy and VNAV gives vertical guidance to more precisely follow specified descent/approach trajectories.

ClearVision

A further option for situational awareness on the ATR 600 Series is Elbit Systems' ClearVision, an enhanced vision system that uses a fuselage-mounted camera to relay high-resolution information and video in real time.

The pilot views the images by wearing a head-mounted visor called Skylens. A synthetic vision system mode provides the pilot's head-up display with digital images of terrain and obstacles, and operators can opt to have a combined vision system blending the enhanced and synthetic modes.

ClearVision-equipped ATRs can take-off and land in low-visibility conditions, making operations possible in conditions that turboprops would otherwise be unable to fly in.

Aurigny and Druk Air in Bhutan have received ClearVision-equipped ATRs. Aurigny ordered the system following a 2018 trial which halved the number of cancelled landings at the airline's Guernsey base due to poor visibility.

New capabilities

Both ATR and Bombardier evolved their respective aircraft during the 2010s. For the Q400 Bombardier introduced extra-capacity cabins with 86 or 90 seats in single class (compared to the standard 82) and a 67-seat dual-class configuration with seven business-class and 60 economy seats.

ATR increased ATR 72-600 capacity from 74 to 78 seats, Cebu Pacific

BELOW • *Deutsche Aircraft plans to fly the D328eco, a refreshed version of the Dornier 328, in 2025.* DEUTSCHE AIRCRAFT

ABOVE • *ATR is planning to introduce the EVO later in the 2020s using new Pratt & Whitney engines.* ATR

introducing the first aircraft so configured in September 2016. It also brought out a revised cabin design with slimline seats, reshaped overhead stowage bins and LED lighting.

Passenger/cargo 'combi' options were developed, offering 50-68 seats and 32m³ volume on the Q400 and 'Cargo Flex' on the ATR 72-600 featuring 44 seats and 19.2m³ volume. Japan Airlines subsidiary Ryukyu Air Commuter introduced the Q400 combi in March 2016 and PNG Airlines the ATR Cargo Flex in 2015.

ATR has introduced new 600 Series variants more recently, most notably a production 72-600 Freighter. FedEx Express Airlines received the first example (EI-GUL c/n 1653) on December 15, 2020, the first in a firm

BELOW RIGHT • *Aurigny ATR 72-600s are equipped with ClearVision to assist in poor-visibility landings.* ATR

order for 30 aircraft plus 20 options placed by the freight giant.

ATR also launched a 42-600 variant optimised for short take-off and landing. The 42-600S first flew on May 11, 2022 from Toulouse-Francazal Airport, France, at which time ATR had 20 commitments from airlines and lessors. The new variant is designed to operate into airports with 800-1,000m runway lengths. Certification testing was under way at the time of writing in September 2023.

Back to the future

A significant change in the turboprops market occurred in 2019 when Bombardier Aerospace, undertaking a significant refocusing of its activities, sold the Dash 8 programme to Longview Aviation Capital.

Longview established a new company, De Havilland Canada (DHC), to produce the aircraft and support older DHC-8-100/-200/-300 variants. The Q400 was rebranded as the DHC-8-400. The new company meant the De Havilland name returned to the commercial aircraft market for the first time in decades.

A sense of 'back to the future' with turboprop airliners was manifested elsewhere in the early 21st century by

several manufacturers updating older types with new engines and avionics.

The Swiss company RUAG acquired the Dornier 228 production rights and type certificate in 2007 and launched the Dornier 228NG (New Generation). Aircraft Industries in Kunovice, Czech Republic (formerly Let) developed the L410NG Turbolet, which flew in 2015.

More recently, at the June 2023 Paris Air Show, DHC announced a plan to restart De Havilland Twin Otter production with a new iteration of the 20-seat turboprop called the DHC-6 Twin Otter Classic 300G. Purchase agreements and letters of intent were announced for 45 aircraft.

The Classic 300G has the same airframe and Pratt & Whitney Canada PT6A turboprops as the legacy Twin Otter but will, DHC says, offer increased payload/range performance and lower operating costs. The aircraft will feature an all-new interior and an updated flightdeck with Garmin G1000 NXi avionics. The Classic 300G is designed for smaller-scale commuter passenger and cargo operations.

Another product for these needs is the Cessna SkyCourier, launched in 2017 by Textron Aviation. This PT6A-65C-powered high-wing, large utility aircraft can seat 19 passengers. It first flew on May 17, 2020 and following US Federal Aviation Administration type certification entered service with FedEx Express Airlines, which has ordered 50, in May 2022.

D328eco

Another refreshed turboprop airliner is the Deutsche Aircraft D328eco, an update of the Dornier 328.

Deutsche Aircraft went public with its plan in 2020. The company was founded by 328 Support Services GmbH (328SSG), the firm that in 2006 purchased the production rights and type certificates for the Dornier

328 (and its short-lived jet derivatives, the 328JET and 528JET) produced by Fairchild Dornier at Oberpfaffenhofen in Germany. The US company Sierra Nevada Corporation acquired 328SSG in 2015.

A May 2023 Deutsche Aircraft statement claimed the D328eco will be "the most efficient, modern and sustainable regional aircraft in its class." It will have an integrated Garmin Companion flightdeck and brand-new PW127XT-S engines designed to operate on 100% sustainable aviation fuel. A first flight is anticipated in 2025.

ABOVE • *Loganair operates both ATR 42s and larger ATR 72s.* LOGANAIR

LEFT • *The Skylens provides an enhanced vision system for the pilot in ATR's ClearVision solution.* ATR

BELOW • *De Havilland Aircraft is to restart DHC-6 Twin Otter, the company announced in June 2023.* DE HAVILLAND AIRCRAFT OF CANADA

Private Wings is the launch customer, having signed a Letter of Intent for five examples. Deutsche Aircraft broke ground on a new factory at Leipzig/Halle Airport in spring 2023 and has announced various supplier agreements including with Liebherr Aerospace, thyssenkrupp, NORDAM and Sasol.

The future

Embraer disclosed in 2020 that it was studying two versions of a proposed new generation turboprop (NGTP) seating 70 to 90 passengers. Building a turboprop airliner would mark a return to the market for the Brazilian company more than 20 years after it ended EMB-120 Brasilia production and focused its commercial airliner activity on regional jets.

A December 2022 Embraer statement to this publication's editor said the company's market studies and discussions with airlines had shown "strong demand exists globally for an advanced next generation turboprop aircraft."

However, the company added, "Embraer has decided to postpone the decision on whether to go ahead" with such a product. It said: "The programme only works if it meets targets on performance, maintenance and sustainability. As of today, the options available from a few suppliers are not yet there with respect to all targets."

Pratt & Whitney and Rolls-Royce have both indicated they have pitched engine options for the NGTP – with P&W reportedly exploring technology developed for its PW127XT engine and Rolls-Royce proposing an all-new powerplant.

Embraer Commercial Aviation president and CEO Arjan Meijer had told the May 2022 Airline Economics forum in Dublin that Embraer was tentatively targeting an entry into service for the NGTP in around 2027/28, assuming an engine selection and the finalisation of the business and

technical cases. Putting the NGTP on ice pushes the service-entry objective beyond then.

Embraer's decision, following the early-2010s choices by both ATR and Bombardier to put on hold proposals for larger 100-seat variants of their aircraft, might suggest the turboprop airliner segment is static. However, with DHC continuing the DHC-8-400 and reviving the Twin Otter and the

forthcoming D328eco, things are happening.

And in May 2022 ATR announced it intends to bring a next generation ATR EVO to market by 2030. The company promised "advanced design features and a new powerplant with hybrid capability" (the PW127XT) offering "significant improvements in performance, economics and sustainability" as well as new avionics and cabin features.

The EVO will offer 20% reductions in fuel burn, carbon dioxide emissions and maintenance costs compared to the current-production ATR 42/72-600, as well as 100% sustainable aviation fuels compatibility and 50% less carbon dioxide emissions compared to a current-generation regional jet, ATR said.

Turboprop airliners are also serving as an entry-point for zero-emissions flight, offering suitable power-to-weight and energy-to-weight characteristics for electric and hydrogen-electric engines.

ABOVE • *Embraer released a CGI of a conceptual Next Generation Turbo Prop in 2021.* EMBRAER

LEFT • *De Havilland Aircraft offers four cargo conversion solutions for its Dash 8-400.* DE HAVILLAND AIRCRAFT OF CANADA

E-Jets E2

Brazil's Embraer has brought out new variants of its regional jet and continues to see bright prospects for the family.

Brazilian manufacturer Embraer launched its E-Jet regional jet family at the June 1999 Paris Air Show. The 72-78-seat E170 was the baseline model, first flying on February 19, 2002, and entering service with LOT Polish Airlines in March 2004.

The slightly stretched E175 with 78-88 seats flew in June 2003 and entered service with Air Canada in July 2005. Further-stretched models then followed – the E190 with 100-114 seats and E195 with 116-124 seats. The first E190 flew in March 2004 and entered service with JetBlue Airways in 2005; the first E195 flew in December 2004 and entered service with Flybe in 2006.

The first-generation E-Jets became a favourite with regional airlines during the 2000s. Embraer's full-year orders and deliveries data for 2024 shows the company had delivered 191 E170s, 568 E190s and 172 E195s (there are currently no orders remaining in the backlog for these variants). Embraer had received orders for 943 E175s of which it has delivered 779.

Enter the E2

The trend of updating proven airliners with more efficient turbofans that led to the A320neo, A330neo, 737 MAX and 777X extended to the regional jets segment of the market.

Embraer launched the E-Jets E2 range at the 2013 Paris Air Show. There are three variants: the baseline E190-E2, stretched E195-E2 and shortened E175-E2 (the smallest

E-Jet, the E170, was not included in the upgrade).

The E190-E2 conducted its maiden flight on May 23, 2016, and entered service with the Norwegian carrier Widerøe on April 24, 2018. The larger E195-E2 took flight on March 29, 2017; Azul Brazilian Airlines introduced it to service on September 12, 2019.

Embraer's latest orders and deliveries data to the end of Q1 2025 shows the company had orders at that point for 52 E190-E2s (it had delivered 27) and 282 E195-E2s (131 delivered). Overall, the E-Jets family had 2,208 firm orders and 1,871 deliveries by the end of the quarter.

PurePower engines

Engines are a principal change between the new models and the first-generation E-Jets. The E1s had General Electric CF34s; the E2s are equipped with the Pratt & Whitney PurePower PW1900G turbofan.

The difference between the fan diameters on the E2s' PW1900G engines (56in on the E175-E2 and 73in on the E190-E2/E195-E2) and those on the first-generation variants' CF34s (53in on the E170/E175 and 57in on the E190/E195) is probably the most notable visual change between the first and second-generation E-Jets.

Another key change between the generations are the E2s' completely redesigned high-aspect ratio wings with raked tips to improve aerodynamic flow. A multidisciplinary process evaluated different wing/pylon/wingtip combinations to find the most efficient design. Other structural changes between the generations are lighter and more robust single-slotted flaps, a new landing gear and tweaks around the airframe to reduce drag.

ABOVE • *Norwegian carrier Widerøe was first to introduce the E2 on April 24, 2018.* EMBRAER

BELOW • *The E190-E2 conducted its maiden flight on May 23, 2016.* EMBRAER

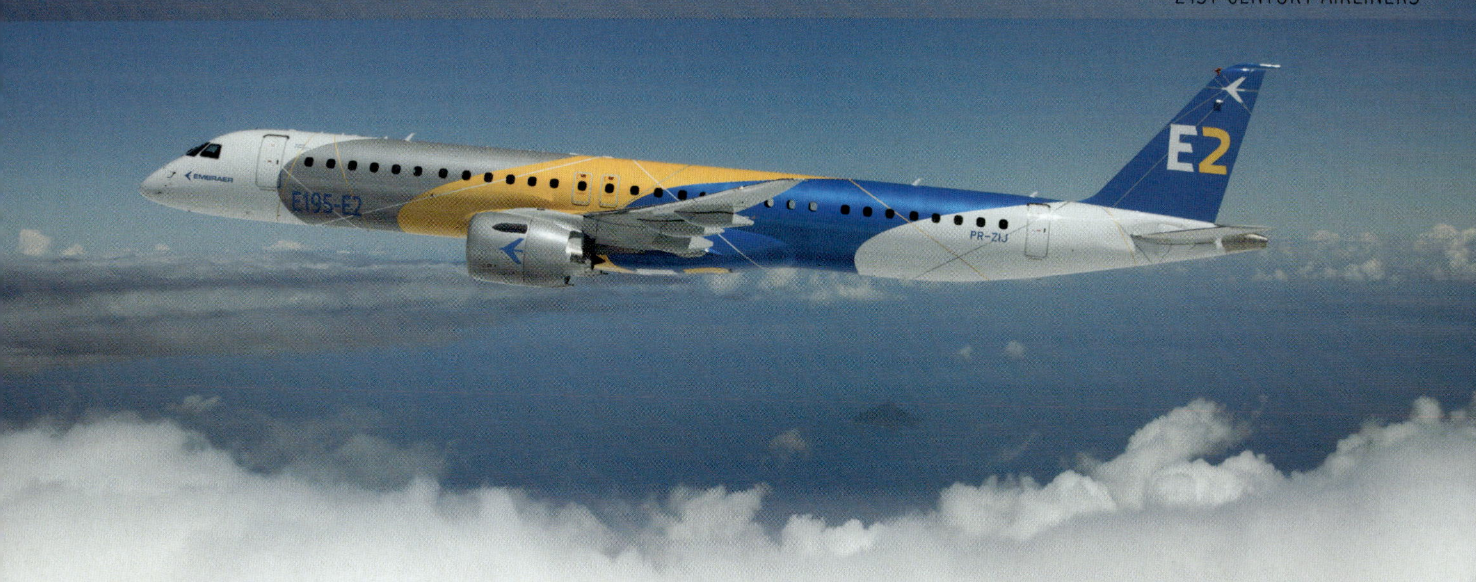

Lower fuel burn

According to Embraer's marketing, the E2 has 25.4% better fuel efficiency per seat and 16% lower fuel consumption compared to the first-generation E-Jet. The aircraft also burn 10% less fuel than competing regional jets, it says. Embraer claims the E2 is "the quietest aircraft in the single-aisle category," generating a 65% smaller noise footprint compared to the E1.

Embraer emphasises peace, quiet and spaciousness when describing the passenger cabin. The E2 has a 2+2 cabin seat layout as standard which, the framer says, "ensures every passenger has more space and comfort to relax in."

The absence of a middle seat also means there's a wider aisle, aiding movement in the cabin and faster boarding and disembarkation. The overhead baggage bins are 40% larger than those in the first-generation aircraft.

Highly efficient HEPA (High Efficiency Particulate Arrestor) filters are standard in the cabin, capturing 99.7% of airborne particles and other biological contaminants as small as 0.3 microns, with cabin air completely refreshed at least 20 times an hour. There is LED mood lighting throughout.

Flightdeck

The E2s have a fully-digital fly-by-wire flight control system. The flight deck has four 13 x 10in full-colour LCD display screens, each 45% larger than the five screens in the E1s. Honeywell Primus Epic 2 integrated avionics have more advanced 3-D graphics and provide more intuitive planning, navigation, and systems management for crews.

The Primus Epic 2 suite also has the SmartView synthetic vision system with SmartRunway and SmartLanding, providing greater situational awareness to pilots during take-off, final approach, landing, and taxiing.

The IntuView weather radar presents a 3-D visualisation of weather around the aircraft and on the route ahead. There is wireless connectivity to enable integration with electronic flight bags.

Despite the changes, Embraer emphasises the E2s maintain commonality with the E1s. To give a couple of examples, the wings are still made from aluminium and the Primus Epic 2 avionics are an evolution of the Primus Epic used in the first-generation aircraft. Type-rated E1 pilots will only need 2.5 days to transition onto an E2 with no full flight simulator or flying time required.

Airlines benefit from longer maintenance intervals than the first-generation jets (at 10,000 flight hours the longest in the single aisle market, Embraer says). The E2's lower fuel burn and carbon dioxide emissions also appeal to those airlines especially sensitive about their sustainable credentials.

KLM Royal Dutch Airlines, for instance, which introduced the E2 in 2022 for its Cityhopper unit flying services from Amsterdam/Schiphol to European cities, said: "The new aircraft type is both quieter and more economical than its predecessor the E190. The E195-E2 uses 9% less fuel per flight and therefore emits 31% less carbon dioxide per passenger in comparison with the E190. This new type is also 63% quieter than the E190."

Freighters

Separate to the E2, in 2022 Embraer launched a freighter

E-Jets E2 operators		
	E190-E2	E195-E2
Air Astana	2	
Air Peace		5
Azul Brazilian Airlines		32
Binter Canarias		14
Helvetic Airways	8	4
Hunnu Air		1
KLM Cityhopper		23
LOT Polish Airlines		3
Pionair Australia	1	
Piacar Linhas Aereas	2	
Porter Airlines		44
Royal Jordanian Airlines	4	2
Scoot	5	
TUIfly Belgium		3
Widerøe	3	

Source: Embraer, correct to May 2025. N.B. no current orders for E175-E2.

TOP • *The larger E195-E2 took flight on March 29, 2017; Azul Brazilian Airlines introduced it to service on September 12, 2019.* EMBRAER

LEFT • *Embraer has painted several E-Jets E2s in special liveries based on the 'Profit Hunter' marketing theme it uses to promote the aircraft, including E190-E2 2-RLET pictured in 2021.* ANA CAROLINE SCHMIDT/ EMBRAER

Embraer E-Jets E2 basic characteristics

	E175-E2	E190-E2	E195-E2
Wingspan	31m (101ft 7in)	33.72m (110ft 6in)	33.72m (110ft 6in)
Length	32.4m (106ft 3in)	36.2m (118ft 11in)	41.5m (136ft 2in)
Height	9.98m (32ft 7in)	10.96m (36ft)	10.91m (35ft 8in)
Maximum fuel capacity	8,522kg (98,120lb)	13,690kg (30,181lb)	13,690kg (30,181lb)
Maximum take-off weight	44,600kg (98,120lb)	56,400kg (124,340lb)	61,500kg (135,585lb)
Seats	80 three-class, 88 or 90 single-class	97 three-class, 106 or 114 single-class	120 three-class, 132 or 140 single-class
Cruise speed	Mach 0.82	Mach 0.82	Mach 0.82
Maximum range	2,000nm (3,704km)	2,850nm (5,275km)	2,600nm (4,815km)
Engines	2x Pratt & Whitney PW1715G generating 15,000lbf (67kN)	2x Pratt & Whitney PW1919G generating 19,000-23,000lbf (85-102kN)	2x Pratt & Whitney PW1919G generating 19,000-23,000lbf (85-102kN)

Source: Embraer

conversion programme for the first-generation E190 and E195 variants, responding to burgeoning demand for more air cargo capacity. Initial deliveries of the initial conversions are planned for 2025.

Embraer said: "Overhead bins are removed, there are new smoke detection and fire suppression systems, the main-deck floor is reinforced and has a cargo handling system, and there is a new forward cargo door."

The converted E190F will have 3,732ft³ volume, 23,600lb total payload and carry seven unit loading device (ULD) pallets on the main deck and underfloor. The E195F will have 4,171ft³ volume, 27,100lb payload and carry eight ULDs. The conversions will offer over 50% more volume capacity and three times the range of large cargo turboprops and up to 30% lower operating costs than narrowbody jets, Embraer says.

The company adds that the E195F will have similar range and payload to the Boeing 737-300SF freighter conversion but consume "less fuel, generate fewer emissions and [have] lower maintenance and cash operating costs." The conversions will bring "right-sizing to the cargo industry by tapping the gap between turboprop and larger narrowbody freighters," it says.

Embraer says: "Cargo airlines can now put right-capacity freighters on the right routes with the right frequency and right economics. Airlines can now access new smaller markets while deploying their larger aircraft on routes where they are more economical."

Embraer forecast in its latest 20-year market outlook a demand for 600 E-Jet freighters over the next 20 years. It said the Chinese market alone is forecast to need 240 aircraft, accounting for 34% of the global total thanks to demand from the e-commerce and logistics sectors.

TOP • *Two of Embraer's demonstrator E-Jets E2s in their promotional liveries.* EMBRAER

LEFT • *The fan diameters on the E2s' PW1900G engines are 56in on the E175-E2 and 73in on the E190-E2/E195-E2.* EMBRAER

ABOVE RIGHT • *Embraer in 2022 launched a freighter conversion programme for the first-generation E190 and E195 variants.* EMBRAER

The company announced an agreement with Lanzhou Aviation Industry Development Group for 20 E190Fs and E195Fs. The two parties intend to cooperate on establishing a E190F/E195F conversion facility in Lanzhou for the introduction of the first-generation E-Jet freighters to the Chinese market.

Scope clauses

Embraer has paused development of the E175-E2 variant. A February 2022 US Securities and Exchange Commission (SEC) filing said the delay is due to "ongoing US mainline scope clause discussions with the pilot unions."

Scope clauses are the agreements in contracts for pilots working for the regional feeder carriers of the big network airlines in the United States that dictate the size and seating configurations of regional aircraft. The E175-E2's 80 seats three-class and 44,600kg (98,120lb) maximum take-off weight exceeds the limits of 76 seats and 86,100lb (39,100kg) in the current scope clauses.

SkyWest Airlines placed a provisional order for 100 aircraft when the E2 programme was launched in anticipation of future amendment to the scope clauses, which have been in place since 2012.

The lack of change, however, meant SkyWest later cancelled the order. Embraer has said it expects to resume the programme development activities for the variant in the future, but the service entry date is now expected no earlier than 2027/28.

In the meantime, orders for the scope-compliant, first-generation E175 continue. Most recently, American Airlines placed a firm order for seven more E175s for its wholly-owned Envoy Air subsidiary. In its SEC filing, Embraer identified "continuing interest in the current E175 jet in the US market."

'Crossover'

Back in 2018, an Embraer spokesperson told this publication's editor it had confidence in the E-Jets E2's future because the family offers "flexibility, versatility and resilience to the cycles inherent in aviation." The subsequent COVID-19 downturn and the post-pandemic recovery was one such cycle.

Embraer sees solid growth for regional aviation. The company's latest 20-year market outlook released at the June 2023 Paris Air Show predicted demand for 11,000 new examples of airliners with up to 150 seats (8,790 regional jets and 2,210 turboprops).

Embraer thinks several trends will drive this demand – more regionalisation of businesses and supply chains, more remote working prompting air services to new communities and the push for sustainability.

In recent years Embraer has called the E-Jet a 'crossover' aircraft in its marketing. The term is familiar in the automotive sector, referring to cars that combine the configurations of a hatchback and an SUV – but what does Embraer mean by it?

A 'crossover' aircraft has between 70 and 150 seats and bridges the higher end of regional aircraft and the lower end of narrowbody types, with configurations that cross between the two categories.

There will be a need, Embraer's market outlook says, "for fleet flexibility to cope with an uncertain and changing demand." It believes the E-Jets E2 variants offer the payload/range flexibility and efficiency across the entire sub-150 seats segment.

BELOW • *The E195-E2 is the most popular E2 variant with more than 200 orders.* EMBRAER

New jets from the East

The 21st century saw new commercial airliners emerge from nations eager to grow their aerospace presence.

China Eastern Airlines introduced the COMAC C919 short-to-medium-haul airliner on May 28, 2023. "China's civil aviation market has got the country's self-developed trunk jetliner," said Wei Yingbiao, vice president of the Commercial Aircraft Corporation of China (COMAC), the C919's developer, according to China's Xinhua news agency. A second China Eastern C919 entered service in July 2023.

LEFT • *The COMAC C919 finally entered commercial service in 2023 after more than a decade in development.* CHINA EASTERN AIRLINES

Development

The C919 was a long time coming. COMAC launched the programme in 2008 and the initial flight test aircraft only conducted its maiden flight from Shanghai Pudong International Airport on May 2, 2017. Five other C919s later joined testing. Civil Aviation Administration of China type certification was received on September 29, 2022.

Various branches of the state-owned Aviation Industry Corporation of China (AVIC) conglomerate, of which COMAC is part, produce C919 structural components. Various Western companies are suppliers including CFM International (LEAP-1C engines), Honeywell (fly-by-wire flight control system, wheels, brakes, auxiliary power unit), GE Aviation (flight deck display screens, onboard maintenance system, flight recorders), Collins Aerospace (avionics) and Liebherr (landing gears).

AVIC Commercial Aircraft Engine (ACAE) integrates the LEAP-1Cs with the C919. A future domestic engine alternative will be the CJ-1000A high-bypass turbofan from ACAE, but its introduction is not expected until the late 2020s/early 2030s.

Market prospects

According to the Xinhua news agency, COMAC has secured orders for more than 1,000 C919s, largely from Chinese leasing companies and banks and the country's largest carriers, Air China, China Eastern Airlines and China Southern Airlines.

The C919 is going up against Airbus A320s and Boeing 737s in China. With airlines generally preferring tried-and-tested equipment backed by comprehensive spares, training, type ratings, maintenance, and in-service support, the C919's appeal beyond China may be restricted – and there is also wider geopolitics to consider.

During the 2000s and 2010s there was a broad move in the West to sell goods and services to China spanning sectors from the motor industry to finance. Western companies supplying the C919 programme was part of this wider trend.

Political relations between China and the West, however, have soured more recently. US and European authorities have tightened export controls and outbound investment to China. They have sought to loosen trade ties, including reducing dependencies on Chinese semiconductors and rare Earths and minerals for batteries. This bigger picture may affect future global export potential for the C919.

SpaceJet cancellation

It took years for the C919 to reach service – and another new airliner from Asia didn't make it that far.

Mitsubishi Aircraft Corporation's parent company Mitsubishi Heavy Industries (MHI) cancelled the SpaceJet on February 7, 2023. In its 2022/23 financial year results presentation, MHI said the aircraft is "not feasible in the market environment."

Mitsubishi had launched the Mitsubishi Regional Jet (MRJ) in March 2008 with two planned versions, a baseline MRJ90 with 86-96 seats and a smaller MRJ70 with 70-80 seats. At this stage, first flight was planned for 2011 and service entry in 2013, but the design was not frozen until mid-2010.

Test flying finally began from Mitsubishi's Nagoya base on November 11, 2015. Four more flight test aircraft followed, with some testing conducted from Grant County International Airport in Washington State, but the development schedule slipped.

At the 2019 Paris Air Show, MHI announced major changes. The MRJ90 was rebranded as the SpaceJet M90 with an amended seat configuration of 81 to 88 seats. Development of the smaller MRJ70 was abandoned in

BELOW • *Mitsubishi Aircraft Corporation's parent company Mitsubishi Heavy Industries (MHI) cancelled the SpaceJet on February 7, 2023.* MITSUBISHI AIRCRAFT

favour of a new smaller variant with 76 seats called the SpaceJet 100.

However, less than 18 months later in late 2020, MHI paused work on the aircraft. And, in the February 2023 notice of the project's cancellation, the company said it had "failed to confirm sufficient business viability for resuming development."

Scope clauses

MHI identified several factors in the programme's cancellation – the protracted development timeline, difficulty in obtaining "understanding and necessary cooperation from global partners," and the challenge of allocating the significant funding required to take the aircraft through the remainder of its testing and into type certification.

Another decisive factor was the issue of scope clauses – the conditions included in agreements between airlines and unions that govern regional airline operations in the United States. Scope clauses specify the size of aircraft US regional carriers can operate and dictate to regional aircraft manufacturers key performance specifications including weight and seat numbers.

ABOVE • *COMAC has secured orders for more than 1,000 C919s mostly from Chinese airlines, leasing companies and banks.* CHINA EASTERN AIRLINES

MHI said: "Little progress on scope clause relaxation resulted in [the] M90 not meeting North American regional jet market needs." Put simply, the SpaceJet was the wrong size.

Mitsubishi Heavy Industries looked for the positives. In its results presentation the company said it had "developed an organisational structure to design, manufacture and certify aircraft which could obtain type certification" and "achieved over 3,900 hours of flight tests with no safety issues."

MHI said it would continue supporting the CRJ regional jet programme, which it acquired from Bombardier in 2020. MHI said in 2021 it may restart production of the CRJ-550, a 50-seat scope clause-compliant CRJ700 variant for US carriers and new-build CRJ700s/900s.

SSJ100 and MC-21

Russia developed new airliners in the early 21st century – the Sukhoi Civil Aircraft Company (SCAC) SSJ-100 regional jet and Irkut MC-21.

The SSJ-100 first flew on May 19, 2008, and entered service with Armavia in 2011. Mostly Russian carriers have introduced the type. In 2018 United Aircraft transferred SCAC and the SSJ-100 from Sukhoi to the Irkut stable.

The MC-21 is a short-to-medium-haul airliner comparable to the A320 and 737 with 132 to 163 seats and 3,500 nautical miles range. The MC-21 first flew on May 28, 2017, and it remains in flight testing.

Western components and systems were supplied for both projects, although cooperation waned after trade sanctions were imposed following Russia's 2014 annexation of Crimea and ended after further international sanctions were imposed against Russia following the invasion of Ukraine in 2022.

The collapse in relations between Russia and the West means Russia is going it alone. Serial production of the SSJ-New, an SSJ-100 with domestic components, is planned to begin in 2024. In August 2023 Irkut changed its name to Yakovlev, reviving the identity of the aircraft design bureaux absorbed into UAC. Reportedly the Yakovlev name will now be used for UAC's airliners.

In 2012 UAC and China's COMAC announced a joint venture to produce the CR929, a 250-to-320-seat widebody airliner. Construction of parts for a first aircraft began in 2021. Uncertainty linked to international sanctions on Russia means COMAC is now pursuing the development independently, *The Air Current* reported during the 2023 Paris Air Show.

LEFT • *Russia's MC-21, in the same market segment as the A320 and 737, first flew on May 28, 2017.* UNITED AIRCRAFT CORPORATION

LEFT • *A 2018 mock-up of the CR929; reportedly China is now pursuing development independently.* UNITED AIRCRAFT CORPORATION

Supersonic age?

Will supersonic commercial flight return, two decades after Concorde last flew? What challenges are there in bringing back high-speed airline flying?

LEFT • *Boom plans to fly Overture in 2027 ahead of service entry two years later.* BOOM SUPERSONIC

BELOW • *Boom Supersonic's Overture will have four non-afterburning high-bypass engines and a gull wing.* BOOM SUPERSONIC

Concorde was futuristic even as it was retired from service in October 2003. Two decades later, there is revived interest in commercial supersonic passenger transport – but a return to truly high-speed passenger flight remains years away.

Aside from the technical task of producing new aircraft and engines for the environment beyond Mach 1, the speed of sound, there is the challenge of making supersonic air travel commercially viable. Tied closely into feasibility is the impact of sonic booms on populated areas.

Boom Supersonic

The Denver, Colorado-based Boom Supersonic is the highest-profile organisation working on a new supersonic airliner. The company hopes to bring its design, Overture, to market in 2029. United Airlines (15 aircraft plus 35 options) and American Airlines (20 plus 40 options) have placed commitments.

Overture will have 65 to 88 seats, a Mach 1.7 cruise speed and 4,250 nautical miles range. Concorde, by comparison, carried 100 passengers, cruised at Mach 2 and had 4,150 miles range.

A factory in the city of Greensboro in North Carolina, due for completion in 2024, will house the final assembly line for Overture. Boom plans to roll out a prototype in 2026 and fly it in 2027.

The initial Overture design featured highly-swept wings and angular underwing engine intakes. Revisions unveiled at Farnborough International 2022 show four non-afterburning high-bypass engines and a gull wing.

In written testimony to the US House of Representatives Transportation Committee in April 2021, Boom CEO Blake Scholl claimed the company is "redefining what it means to travel long distances."

Scholl wrote: "We envision a future in which anyone can buy a ticket and enjoy the benefits of high-speed travel. Aboard Overture, London would be just 3.5 hours from New York, and Sydney becomes as accessible as Honolulu is today. With Overture, three-day business trips could be done in just one day."

In June 2023, Boom announced agreements with Aernnova for Overture's wings, Leonardo for the fuselage and wing box, and Aciturri for the empennage. Safran Landing Systems, Eaton, Collins Aerospace, Flight Safety International, Florida Turbine Technologies (FTT), GE Additive and StandardAero are other suppliers.

Boom initially planned to develop an engine for Overture with Rolls-Royce,

ABOVE • *The NASA X-59 will fly over US communities to gather data on responses to quiet supersonic technology.* NASA

BELOW LEFT • *NASA image of how it expects the X-59's elongated shape to distribute the shockwave around the aircraft.* NASA

BELOW RIGHT • *NASA uses Schlieren photography to image shockwaves from its rockets and aircraft, as here with a T-38 Talon.* NASA

nautical miles to slow from Mach 2 to subsonic. Add to that the 50nm to compensate for our thrown-forward boom and we were looking at a point 155nm from landfall." On the eastern side of the Atlantic Ocean, Concorde only accelerated to supersonic speed over the Bristol Channel and southern Ireland.

Another issue for Concorde was the noise impact on communities from its Rolls-Royce Olympus engines on take-off and landing. Boom Supersonic's Blake Scholl wrote in his 2021 Transportation Committee testimony: "Our team is working to maximise efficiency and minimise noise in Overture's design."

Early in 2025 Boom said its XB-1 had flown supersonically over land with no audible boom. The company announced what it calls 'Boomless Cruise' – the concept of flying at a sufficiently high altitude at an appropriate speed for current atmospheric conditions to ensure a sonic boom never reaches the ground.

NASA X-59

On the issue of quiet supersonic flight, NASA's Quesst mission has two goals. Its first objective is to design and build a research aircraft with technology that reduces the loudness of a sonic boom to people on the ground to a gentle 'thump' sound. The second is to fly the aircraft over land to gather data on human responses to the sound and deliver the data set to US and international regulators.

The resulting research aircraft is the X-59, built by Lockheed Martin at its Skunk Works facility in Palmdale, California. NASA test pilots will fly this highly streamlined machine at supersonic speeds above US communities from 2024.

The aircraft will gather the data the FAA will need to decide whether to change the half-century-long prohibition on overland supersonic flight – a pivotal decision in the future for a new supersonic age.

An April 2023 NASA statement explained: "To lift the ban and enable a viable market for supersonic air travel over land, the idea is that regulators would base new rules on a different standard than before. The speed limit created in 1973 didn't consider the possibility that an airplane could fly supersonic yet did not create sonic booms that could affect anyone below. It was a fair assessment at the time because the technology required to make that happen didn't exist yet."

Peter Coen, NASA's Quesst mission integration manager, said: "Instead of a rule based solely on speed, we are proposing the rule be based on sound. If the sound of a supersonic flight isn't loud enough to bother anyone below, there's no reason why the airplane can't be flying supersonic."

Shockwave

NASA says the way shockwaves will form around the X-59 will differ from what the agency calls a 'conventional supersonic aircraft'.

On older aircraft, it says, multiple shockwaves merged together. The sleek X-59's noticeably long and thin nose, however, "pierces through the air – a key design for quieting the boom," NASA says.

Essentially, the long nose 'stretches' air molecules around the aircraft so the waves do not fully merge and are instead spread out. The thinking is the sound heard on the ground below the X-59 will be a quieter 'thump' rather than a loud boom.

So streamlined is the dart-like X-59 that the aircraft's single pilot will not have a forward-facing window. Instead, a 4K/ultra-HD monitor developed by the NASA Langley Research Center will serve as the central 'window' enabling them to see their flight path while viewing flight data in augmented reality.

A computational fluid dynamics illustration released by NASA in April 2023, visualising the shockwaves coming off the X-59, was used in creating the flight planning tools and software for Quesst.

Researchers from NASA's Armstrong Flight Research Center at Edwards Air Force Base, California, which is managing the X-59 flight test campaign, will capture images of the shockwaves the X-59 generates using a specialist technique used by NASA to photograph shockwaves from its rockets and aircraft.

Schlieren photography uses a textured background, such as the edge of the Sun or sunspots, to visualise changes in air density. As light flows around an object, the change in air density caused by the airflow bends the light, making the edge of the Sun and sunspots appear to move. Software then calculates how each spot moved to reconstruct the shockwave into an image.

Ed Haering, principal investigator for the Schlieren photography at

NASA Armstrong, said in December 2022: "We want to be able to have a proven system to be able to image the shockwaves. That way we can have proof of the shockwave distribution around the X-59 that hopefully will result in the quiet thump on the ground."

By September 2023 major structural assembly of the X-59 was complete and system check-out tests under way. Painting and rollout were planned for autumn 2023 ahead of the first flight.

Speed premium

Concorde generated revenue for British Airways – but can an airline with supersonic aircraft make it work today?

Much of the Anglo-French aircraft's circa £2 billion development cost (1976 prices) was written off. Spike Aerospace indicates the development costs involved with supersonic aircraft development by mentioning on its website that the estimated unit price of an S-512 will be $100 million.

Any future supersonic (or hypersonic) commercial aircraft will serve the higher end of the air passenger market for business travellers, continuing the trend from the Concorde era when, Mike Bannister points out in his autobiography, 80% of passengers were businesspeople (the remainder was 10% rich and famous, 5% sportspeople and 5% trip-of-a-lifetime).

The speed premium of Concorde – the aircraft flew faster than the Earth rotates and faster than a rifle bullet – was its selling point, enabling its clientele to wake up in London and get to New York for a morning meeting.

Commercial airliners typically cruise at Mach 0.85. Top-of-the-range business jets are slightly faster – the Bombardier Global 6500 and Dassault Falcon 7X/8X cruise at Mach 0.90 and the Global 7500/8000 and Gulfstream G650/650ER can reach Mach 0.92.

Supersonic/hypersonic aircraft developers hope their designs, by surpassing these speeds, will make a difference to the time-pressed business traveller. A 2021 Boom Supersonic statement says Overture will be able to "connect more than 500 destinations in nearly half the time" as a subsonic airliner. Spike says its S-512 will cut New York-London travel times to 3.3 hours and London-Dubai to 3.2 hours. Destinus says its hypersonic design would cut the journey from Paris to New York to just 90 minutes.

Supersonic air travel however was not simply about the flight time. A comfortable experience matters – as BA showed with Concorde's high-quality food, fine wines and stellar onboard service. Spike Aerospace claims its S-512 will offer "luxury accommodation for productivity or pleasure."

United and American signing for Boom Overtures (at least provisionally) suggests some carriers see a market – albeit a niche one – of well-heeled travellers willing to pay a premium for ultrafast, luxurious connectivity.

Halo effect?

There could be a potential reputational benefit for operators. British Airways cited a 'halo effect' from offering supersonic services. "Without Concorde, we would have been another airline. Thanks to her, we'd been an airline apart," Bannister says.

On the other hand, broadband connectivity means travellers can conduct business in flight even if they are flying at subsonic speeds – indeed, the rise of services such as Zoom and Microsoft Teams might mean they may not even have to make a journey at all.

In 2021, *Forbes*' Dan Reed wrote: "Are those savings generated by the executive flying supersonically enough to justify the way higher costs? In many, maybe even most, cases the real answer is likely to be 'no'."

Operating supersonic airliners might pose other issues. John Strickland, the managing director of JLS Consulting who worked at BA when Concorde was in its heyday, remarked: "Even then, there were challenges."

He explained: "New York of course was key but with other US points like Miami and Washington, DC there was not enough demand to make things profitable. Even New York is not the same all year round in business traffic. We had small seasonal operations like Barbados, but it was only a couple of flights a week."

There were only certain routes and times where Concorde worked, Strickland says: "You have times where there isn't demand, so what do you with your planes then?" Operators will need to have a granular understanding of travel market characteristics and routes their aircraft might serve.

And this is why the issue of overland supersonic flight and noise matters. Allowing it will give airlines much more flexibility about routes and make it cost-effective to operate supersonic aircraft.

A supersonic network might bring logistical challenges, however. Strickland points out that having Concorde operations focused at London/Heathrow was advantageous for BA in providing comprehensive engineering support and spare aircraft availability. "Splitting an already small fleet may not be ideal," he says.

Sustainability

There is another fundamental issue – sustainability. Strickland notes: "There is concern about [supersonic] aircraft flying higher than current [subsonic] airliners. Emissions is such a big issue."

Developers stress their environmental credentials. Boom Supersonic, for example, says the Symphony engine for Overture will be optimised for 100% sustainable aviation fuels and feature a single-stage fan "designed for quiet operation." Destinus says its hypersonic design will use hydrogen fuel.

Strickland notes the environment "wasn't really around in Concorde's day" quite how it is today in the corporate world. Environmental, social and governance (ESG) criteria is prominent.

Crucially, business investment decisions are increasingly linked to sustainability. For example, Rob Desborough, managing partner and CEO of the commercial space venture capital fund Seraphim, told the 2022 Royal Aeronautical Society New Space Conference that when the company floated on the London Stock Exchange in 2021: "It was the first question from the capital markets – 'what are you doing from an ESG perspective?'."

For all the glamour of supersonic flight, does it really align with modern times? The issue of how supersonic flight fits with wider business trends could be an issue in it becoming an everyday reality. Companies may "have been previous customers for a fast supersonic airliner – now they may not," Strickland observes. Any new thoroughbred supersonic aircraft will have to be sustainable as well as speedy.

High hopes

How can hydrogen help the efforts to decarbonise aviation? What are the issues surrounding the technology?

Hydrogen became a notable research/development area in the aerospace industry in the early 2020s. Under its ZEROe initiative, Airbus researched a blended wing body, a turbojet and a turboprop using either liquid hydrogen or hydrogen fuel cells. During the March 2025 Airbus Summit event in Toulouse, the company announced it had down-selected fuel cells for a conceptual 100-seat hydrogen airliner.

This notional aircraft has four two-megawatt (MW) electric propulsion engines. Each powerplant will use a hydrogen fuel cell stack. Liquid hydrogen for the cells will be transferred from two cryogenic tanks aboard. A chemical reaction between the hydrogen and oxygen will generate electrical energy to power each engine.

Airbus said: "The only byproduct of this reaction will be water, meaning the process will be almost carbon neutral as long as the hydrogen is made using renewable energy. There will be four propellers, each powered by its own fuel cell stack."

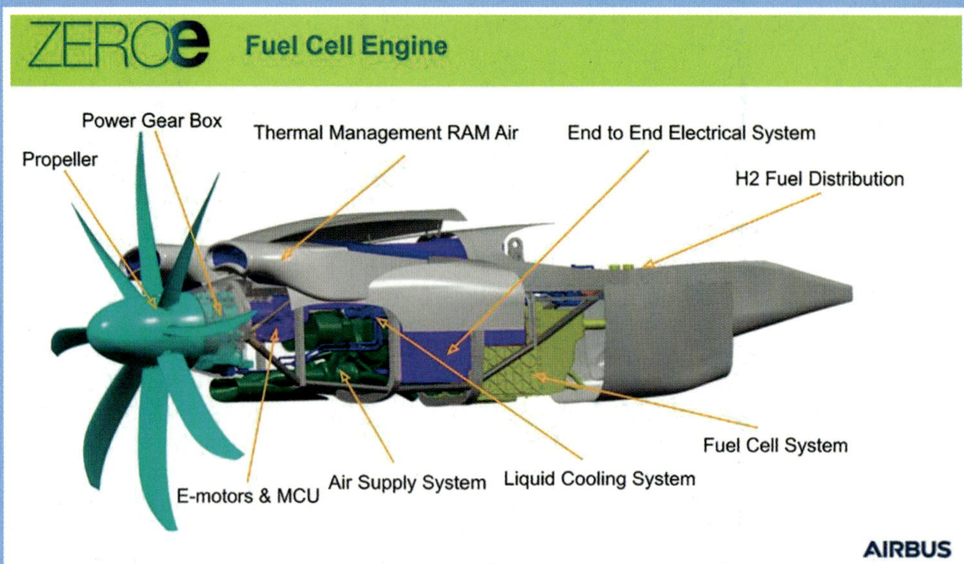

Airbus' head of the ZEROe project, Glenn Llewellyn, commented: "We are confident it could provide the necessary power density for a hydrogen-powered commercial aircraft and could evolve as we mature the technology."

Airbus said its concept "will continue to be refined over the coming years" with additional tests on propulsion systems and technologies associated with hydrogen storage and distribution.

Scalable power

Hydrogen fuel cells convert energy in hydrogen and oxygen molecules into electricity using an electrochemical reaction. Airbus says the cells are "highly efficient" and "can operate continuously, as long as a constant supply of hydrogen is ensured."

In previously released marketing material, Airbus said hydrogen is lighter than conventional Jet-A aviation fuel

ABOVE • *A breakdown of Airbus ZEROe hydrogen-powered fuel cell engine, element per element.* AIRBUS

BELOW • *The pushback to the ZEROe project timeline reflects the challenges in hydrogen technology development.* AIRBUS

ABOVE • *Airbus has ditched turbofan and blended wing configurations to focus on a turboprop using hydrogen fuel cells.* AIRBUS

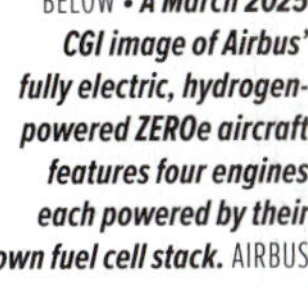

BELOW • *A March 2025 CGI image of Airbus' fully electric, hydrogen-powered ZEROe aircraft features four engines each powered by their own fuel cell stack.* AIRBUS

for a given volume of energy. Hydrogen also raises the possibility of eliminating carbon dioxide emissions. Multiple hydrogen cells connected to create a fuel cell 'stack' will, Airbus says, enable "scalable power generation."

The International Air Transport Association noted: "Hydrogen aircraft have been studied for decades but have never been certified to transport passengers. Earlier tests include NACA's B-57B hydrogen test flight in the 1950s, Tupolev's Tu-155 flight in the 1980s, and more recently, Boeing's six technology demonstrations with crewed and uncrewed aircraft."

IATA said: "Recent pressure for more environmentally friendly flying (to reduce both carbon dioxide [CO2] and non-CO2 emissions) and a recognition of the system-level requirements for decarbonising aviation, have resulted in strong investor interest in developing the technologies required to make this a reality."

ZEROe research

IATA noted, however, there are no commercially available hydrogen fuel cells "large enough to power an aircraft while remaining at an acceptable weight for flight."

Producing a hydrogen-powered airliner will involve considerable technical work. A commercially viable fuel cell must offer good performance, low weight, and meet aerospace safety regulations.

Airbus is investigating how to address these issues with R&D projects as part of ZEROe. Its Aerostack joint venture with ElringKlinger in 2023 undertook extensive testing on a prototype hydrogen fuel cell using Airbus' E-Aircraft System House at Ottobrunn near Munich. The cell reached its 1.2MW full-power level, which Airbus said is "the most powerful test ever achieved in aviation of a fuel cell designed for large-scale aircraft."

A hydrogen propulsion system also includes a propeller, an electrically driven motor and motor control unit, a power gear box, and systems for fuel distribution, air supply, thermal management, liquid cooling and electrical power.

The ZEROe research integrated the fuel cell with the electrical motor to measure how the propulsion system works in different flight phases, from take-off where maximum power is required to cruise where less power is needed.

The electric motors were 'powered on' with the hydrogen fuel cells for the first time at the end of 2023. Hauke Peer-Luedders, head of fuel cell propulsion for ZEROe, said: "Observing how the many systems interact enables engineers to see what changes need to be made to make the technology flight-worthy."

Airbus, in collaboration with Air Liquide Advanced Technologies, has also developed the Liquid Hydrogen BreadBoard in Grenoble, France to investigate hydrogen storage, distribution and propulsion systems.

Airbus said: "Integrated ground testing is planned for 2027 at the Electric Aircraft System Test House in Munich, combining the propulsive

bench and hydrogen distribution system for comprehensive system validation."

Another aircraft manufacturer, Embraer, launched its Energia project in 2021 to study hydrogen fuel cells and liquid hydrogen for conceptual low-emissions regional aircraft.

In an update during Embraer's annual investor day in November 2024, the company's vice-president of engineering and technology development, Luis Carlos Affonso, said the pace of technology development means an Embraer hydrogen-powered aircraft is now more likely in the 2040s than the 2030s.

ZeroAvia

In 2023, the UK/US start-up ZeroAvia flew its 19-seat Dornier 228 demonstrator (G-HFZA c/n 8046) retrofitted with the company's full-size prototype ZA600 hydrogen-electric powertrain, from Cotswold Airport at Kemble, Gloucestershire. The company later presented what it calls its "breakthrough" multi-megawatt modular electric motor system in a more powerful 1.8MW prototype configuration.

ZeroAvia said in February 2025: "The company has an engineering partnership with Textron Aviation as it looks to secure a supplemental type certificate for the Cessna Grand Caravan as the launch airframe for the ZA600."

ZeroAvia has also tested technologies for a larger powertrain, the ZA2000, including cryogenic tanks housing liquid hydrogen and proprietary high-temperature fuel cell and electric propulsion systems. The ZA2000 is designed to support 80-seat regional turboprop aircraft such as the ATR 72 and the Dash 8-400.

On May 21, 2025 ZeroAvia announced that it will build a major manufacturing facility for production of its hydrogen-

electric powertrains at the Advanced Manufacturing Innovation District Scotland, close to Glasgow Airport in Renfrewshire.

At the June 2023 Paris Air Show, ZeroAvia said it had identified "clear applications" for hydrogen-electric propulsion for regional jets. The company announced an initial technical study with MHI RJ Aviation (the type certificate holder for the CRJ regional jet), which identified "an initial entry-point for a CRJ 700 retrofit with ZeroAvia's ZA2000RJ powertrain" and "validates the retrofit approach for other in-service CRJ series aircraft, such as the CRJ 550 and CRJ 900."

ZeroAvia explained: "The hydrogen-electric CRJ aircraft would be equipped with two ZeroAvia regional jet engines (derivatives of the ZA2000 engine class) to match the existing performance and ZeroAvia analysis suggests it could support up to 60 passengers with a range of up to 560 nautical miles, covering in excess of 80% of current flights."

Dorniers and Islander

Other organisations exploring hydrogen include Stuttgart, Germany-based H2FLY, whose HY4 demonstrator (S5-MHY) completed the world's first piloted flight of an electric aircraft powered by liquid hydrogen from Maribor Airport in Slovenia in September 2023.

The German Aerospace Center (Deutsches Zentrum für Luft- und Raumfahrt; DLR) will use a leased Dornier 328-100 Model 20 D-CUPL (c/n 3061) as a flying testbed for hydrogen technologies. MTU Aero Engines plans to fly a Dornier 228 with a hydrogen powertrain by 2026.

Britten-Norman and Cranfield Aerospace Solutions are working on a hydrogen-electric fuel cell for the BN-2

Islander under its Project Fresson initiative. The initial converted Islander was G-HYUK (c/n 2272), which in an earlier guise as G-BUBP was in the James Bond film *Spectre*.

However, this project is seemingly delayed. The hydrogen Islander's first post-conversion flight was expected in late 2023/early 2024 with service entry planned for 2026 following certification, but at the time of writing in spring 2025 the aircraft had yet to fly.

In February 2025, the UK Civil Aviation Authority announced the extension of its Hydrogen Challenge studying hydrogen propulsion, airport infrastructure development and aircraft systems. Cranfield Aerospace Solutions will use their Islander to test potential regulations for hydrogen fuel cell electric propulsion systems.

'Not yet there'

When it launched the ZEROe project, Airbus said it wanted to introduce a hydrogen-powered airliner in the mid-2030s. During the March 2025 Airbus Summit, the company announced a "revised project roadmap."

The manufacturer did not disclose a specific timeline, but the company said more time is required "to mature the technologies." Some reports suggest the service-entry target has been knocked back by as much as ten years – meaning an Airbus hydrogen airliner is unlikely until the mid-2040s at the very earliest.

Commenting on the revised timeline, Airbus CEO Guillaume Faury said during the summit: "We've learned a lot. We've learned we can develop a commercial hydrogen plane that works. We've learned as well that the competitiveness of such a plane would

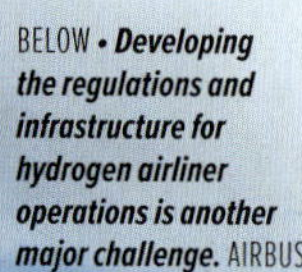

LEFT • Work under way at the Airbus and Air Liquide Liquid Hydrogen Breadboard facility in Grenoble, France testing hydrogen storage and distribution. AIRBUS

BELOW • Developing the regulations and infrastructure for hydrogen airliner operations is another major challenge. AIRBUS

ABOVE • *Airbus' latest ZEROe configuration features two liquid hydrogen tanks located at the rear of the fuselage.*
AIRBUS

not be good enough to compete with the other planes."

Faury said if Airbus had decided to proceed with a hydrogen aircraft just now, in the mid-2020s, "we would have a risk of a 'Concorde of hydrogen' where we would have a solution, but not a commercially viable solution at scale. We're not yet there."

Considerable technology, regulatory and infrastructure challenges around hydrogen have led to the timeline change, which broadly puts the project in line with IATA expectations of a mid-century introduction of hydrogen airliners.

Storage is foremost among the challenges. A 2023 Air BP blog noted: "A redesign of much of the aircraft from the propulsion system to fuel storage is necessary."

Bernard van Dijk, a lecturer at Amsterdam University of Applied Sciences, said in a November 2022 online presentation that four times more hydrogen is required in volume as Jet-A for the same amount of energy, meaning a hydrogen-powered aircraft will require large storage tanks.

An analysis from the ICF consultancy explained: "The comparative advantage of hydrogen diminishes at longer ranges, both because the volume needed to store the hydrogen becomes prohibitive, and because the efficiency advantage is smaller when compared to the higher bypass and pressure ratio of the larger engines on widebody aircraft."

Manufacturers will have to work through trade-offs between energy density, payload/range performance

and efficiency to produce cost-effective and practical configurations. Hydrogen-powered aircraft will also need to achieve equivalent, or better, safety levels than current, conventionally powered aircraft.

Creating cost-effective hydrogen aircraft will inevitably be costly, and the journey has already seen one start-up fall by the wayside.

Universal Hydrogen worked on a regional aircraft conversion carrying hydrogen aboard in proprietary, lightweight, modular capsules. Despite receiving orders and starting flight testing in 2023 from Mojave Air and Space Port in California using a converted De Havilland Canada DHC-8-300 nicknamed *Lightning McClean* (N330EN c/n 274), Universal Hydrogen shut down in 2024.

'Green' hydrogen

There are other significant issues. Although hydrogen is abundant in oceans, rivers, lakes and the atmosphere, chemical synthesis is required to turn it into a fuel.

ICF explains: "Synthetic fuels require a source of carbon, which must be directly extracted from the atmosphere to be sustainable, and there are considerable energy losses incurred during the conversion from hydrogen to a liquid fuel."

According to the International Energy Agency (IEA), 94 megatonnes of hydrogen was produced in 2021 to satisfy demand from heavy industries, including chemical processing, steel production and oil refining.

However, the IEA says, only 1% of global hydrogen was 'low-emission' – and it was mostly produced "from unabated fossil fuels, with deleterious effects on the climate."

ICF notes: "The most common production process is steam methane reforming of natural gas...The second most common uses coal as a feedstock and is even worse from an environmental perspective."

It adds: "The remaining production methods either capture and sequestrate the carbon or create the hydrogen using clean renewable power. While this improves their environmental credentials, it also adds considerable cost."

Producing 'green' hydrogen (that is, fuel manufactured using renewable power such as solar and wind) is the solution, but scaling-up production to increase availability is far more expensive than producing conventional jet fuel.

ABOVE • *In June 2023 ZeroAvia said it has identified an initial entry-point for a CRJ 700 retrofitted with hydrogen technology.* ZEROAVIA

ICF believes the aviation sector has only 'limited' ability to drive transition by itself: "It will be reliant on governments and other larger industries to stimulate the cycle of increasing scale and cost reductions past the early tipping points."

Infrastructure

The logistics involved with hydrogen fuel pose a further challenge. Amsterdam University's Bernard van Dijk said hydrogen requires 2.4 times higher pressure than Jet-A fuel to distribute.

Existing pipelines are not designed to transport hydrogen fuel, so significant changes are required to airport and refuelling infrastructure, with entirely new or modified pipelines and specialist vehicles and equipment. The aviation industry will have to invest extensively in new infrastructure to safely supply, store and move hydrogen. New cross-industry safety standards, protocols and handling procedures are needed.

And the ICF analysis notes hydrogen production would "require significant renewable energy available within a reasonable distance from the airport" to make it 'green' and cost-effective. This, it says, "necessitates large amounts of land and natural resources such as sun and wind – not always available around airports."

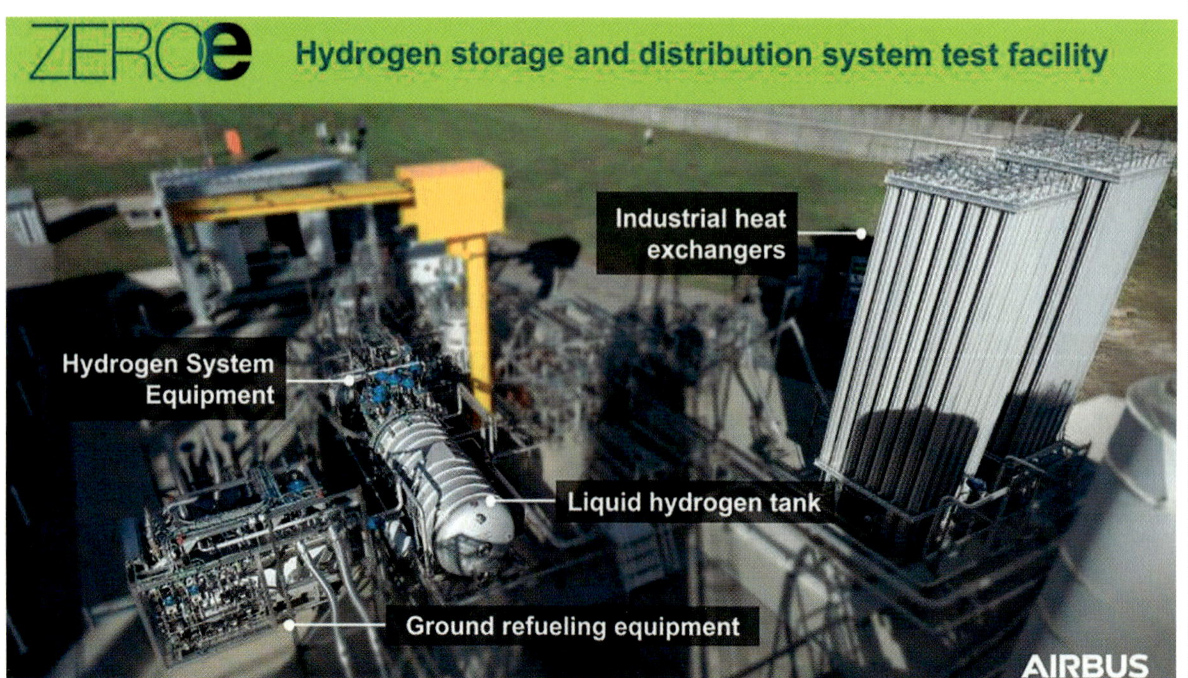

LEFT • *The ZEROe hydrogen storage and distribution system test facility.* AIRBUS

BELOW • *ZeroAvia flew its ZA600 powertrain aboard a Dornier 228 from Kemble.* ZEROAVIA

Initiatives are under way to explore how to bring hydrogen into the aviation ecosystem. The HYPORT project plans to advance hydrogen fuel operations research by developing a prototype liquid-hydrogen refuelling station at Toulouse-Blagnac Airport in France.

Airbus has its Hydrogen Hubs at Airports programme which "brings together airlines, airports, industry players, energy providers and technology specialists to address the key questions around producing, storing and distributing hydrogen."

This programme currently counts more than 220 airports as partners, along with energy providers (including Air Liquide, Air Products, Plug and Repsol) and airlines like Delta, easyJet and Lufthansa.

Manchester Airport intends to become the first UK airport with a direct liquid-hydrogen fuel supply through a link to HyNet, a new underground hydrogen fuel pipeline in northwest England planned for the late 2020s. London/Gatwick and Leeds Bradford airports are working with UK clean energy company ITM Power to develop on-site hydrogen production facilities to fuel airport ground vehicles including tugs and buses.

In September 2023, several companies in the UK aviation and renewable energy sectors including easyJet, Rolls-Royce, Airbus, Ørsted, GKN Aerospace and Bristol Airport established the Hydrogen in Aviation alliance.

Longer term, ICF foresees a "potential bottleneck" in certification: "Clear processes supported by adequate resources will be necessary to ensure new technologies can enter the market quickly and safely."

'Years away'

The multiple challenges with hydrogen are why some observers question the true viability of the fuel for aviation.

Amsterdam University's Bernard van Dijk is a member of the Hydrogen Science Coalition, which describes itself as "a group of independent academics, scientists and engineers who are working to bring an evidence-based viewpoint to the heart of the hydrogen discussion".

In his November 2022 online presentation, van Dijk said "enormous amounts of green electricity" are needed to produce the large fuel volumes aviation requires. Issues of storing the fuel aboard aircraft would reduce aircraft payloads by 15-40% from current types depending on the range flown, he said.

ICF's analysis noted the "high upfront costs" and "significant development risks" involved, and said future opportunities are "many years away."

There are those who say the challenges of scaling hydrogen are too formidable – and therefore not worth trying to overcome at the expense of pursuing other means of cleaning up aviation, such as sustainable aviation fuels. Blake Scholl, founder and CEO of Boom Supersonic, said in an April 21, 2025 post on X: "It's good to see Airbus backing off on hydrogen. There are much better decarbonisation options for aviation."

Nevertheless, said Airbus head of future programmes Bruno Fichefeux during the 2025 Airbus Summit, the company has an "unwavering" commitment to hydrogen-powered flight.

Swiss aviator Bertrand Piccard, who flew around the world using the Solar Impulse electric aircraft in 2015, and whose Climate Impulse project now aims to fly the first aircraft non-stop around the world powered entirely by 'green' hydrogen, said: "It's not more difficult than what has been achieved in the past. It's a question of getting all the actors aligned. You might think hydrogen is science fiction. It's not more science fiction than the Wright Brothers in 1903."

Airbus' Faury acknowledged a hydrogen airliner "is not around the corner" but said: "Still we remain committed. Hydrogen has a role to play. It is an energy of the future."

Future airliners

New engines, electric airliners, sustainable fuels, and cutting-edge technology are all under development for the commercial aircraft of tomorrow.

In the near term, new airliners are likely to be further iterations of existing designs.

Airbus for example is looking at a third A220 variant. During the 2023 Paris Air Show, Airbus' chief commercial officer at the time, Christian Scherer confirmed the company was considering different engine options and revisions to the aircraft's carbon-fibre construction, including the wing.

Exact timing was unclear at the time of writing in May 2025, although the development cycles typical for airliners in the 21st century indicates a 2028/29 service-entry date.

Looking ahead

What other airliners are likely to arrive? In the 2010s it seemed the next Boeing commercial type might be an aircraft sized between the smallest widebodies and the largest narrowbodies.

Boeing studied a New Mid-market Airplane (NMA) concept for a jet with around 220-300 seats and 5,000 nautical miles range. An NMA could have arrived during the 2020s – but with its focus on 777X development and responding to the 737 MAX disasters, Boeing paused the studies. It remains to be seen if there will be any further activity with midsize aircraft. Airbus' latest longer-range A321 derivatives have secured hundreds of orders from carriers seeking replacements for ageing types such as Boeing 757s serving this market segment.

For the two major aircraft manufacturers, a wider product-development decision looms from along the road – the task of developing replacements for the big-selling single-aisle airliner families that form the bedrock of their businesses. Boeing and Airbus still have thousands of these aircraft left to deliver and years of production ahead, however at some stage the companies will have to produce new-generation successors.

Airbus said during its March 2025 summit in Toulouse such an aircraft "could enter service in the second half of the 2030s". Open rotor fan engines, long foldable wings for aerodynamic gains, next-generation batteries, lightweight materials and integrated systems could all feature.

While looking to the future, aircraft manufacturers also must ensure they deliver the aircraft from those already-bulging orderbooks – and an important near-term task there is tackling supply chain difficulties that

BELOW • *Efforts are under way across aerospace to harness new technology to improve environmental performance.* UK AEROSPACE TECHNOLOGY INSTITUTE

Graphene

Manchester is a pioneering city in engineering and technology. Two hundred years ago it was in the heart of Britain's Industrial Revolution. In the 20th century Ernest Rutherford split the atom there and it was home to the first programmable computer.

Two University of Manchester researchers, Professors Andre Geim and Konstantin Novoselov, continued the innovative trend in 2004 by discovering a new super-material called graphene. They were awarded the Nobel Prize for Physics in 2010 for the achievement.

The university opened the National Graphene Institute in 2015 to lead research and the Graphene Engineering Innovation Centre in 2018 to lead industrialisation.

Graphene is the thinnest material ever made – it is a sheet of carbon just one atom thick. It has been hailed as a modern wonder, ultra-light yet stronger than steel, malleable and electrically and thermally conducive. Its characteristics offer potential in fields ranging from energy and electronics to chemicals and medicine.

A 2018 UK Aerospace Technology Institute paper highlighted graphene's promise for aviation – which includes using it for sensors, energy storage, electronics, and manufacturing. It can also be used in conjunction with other advanced materials such as carbon fibre to enhance components. In 2018 the partners of the Graphene Flagship, a pan-European project, developed a 'graphene-enhanced' leading edge for an A350 horizontal tailplane.

ABOVE • *Airbus is researched blended wings as part of the ZEROe project.* AIRBUS

have seriously disrupted production in recent years.

Sustainability push

Whatever manufacturers' future decisions, they will have to be in lockstep with sustainability.

In October 2021 the International Civil Aviation Organization set a formidable target for the aviation industry – achieving net-zero carbon dioxide emissions by 2050, bringing air transport in line with the 2015 Paris Agreement to limit the global average temperature increase to below 2°C by mid-century.

To help provide guidance to the industry, the International Air Transport Association (IATA) in June 2023 issued roadmaps covering aircraft/engine technology, energy/fuels, finance, operations, and policy.

IATA says in one roadmap: "Historically, new-generation aircraft have delivered a 20% reduction in energy use compared to the aircraft they replace…Recent technology assessments for evolutionary aircraft predict another 15-20% improvement compared to the best technology available today."

There are various ways the industry can improve aircraft, engines, and systems. They can modernise production methods to create lighter and more integrated structures by using new techniques such as additive manufacturing, and more extensively use advanced materials such as carbon fibre composites. Materials development itself is another avenue, from increasing the effectiveness of composites to exploring the possibilities of exotic new materials like graphene (see panel) and even bio-sourced resins and natural fibres.

New wings

Evolving aircraft aerodynamics is a large area. The German Aerospace Center (DLR, Deutsches Zentrum für Luft- und Raumfahrt), for example, is investigating an 'intelligent wing' (INTELWI) with active and passive load sensors that respond autonomously to manoeuvres and gusts to improve efficiency. The DLR's webpage on INTELWI lists Airbus as a project partner.

Airbus has its own in-house aerodynamics research. The company's UpNext subsidiary is set to flight-test various technologies – including gust sensors, pop-up spoilers and multifunctional trailing edges – in the eXtra Performance Wing project using a Cessna Citation VII business jet.

A separate Airbus project, Wing of

Tomorrow, is investigating aerodynamic improvements, new wing architectures, composite materials, and manufacturing improvements. Three prototype wings will assess systems integration, compare test data against computer modelling and industrial scale-up.

Aspect ratio is a wing's thickness relative to its span. Engineers refer to the combination of short distance between a wing's leading and trailing edges (known technically as a short chord) and a long wingspan as a high aspect ratio.

Aircraft with a high-aspect ratio wing tend to have low vehicle-induced drag, which improves lift characteristics. This efficiency advantage is why gliders have long and narrow wings.

The UK Aerospace Technology Institute investigated a new composite, high-aspect ratio wing "optimised for aerodynamic efficiency and rapid assembly." The institute's 2022 development roadmap says: "We aim to achieve at least 10% efficiency improvement with over 15% weight reduction and over 10% aerodynamic improvement for the next generation of aircraft."

Towards the X-66A

Extended length means high-aspect ratio wings are susceptible to flutter, or flexing. A joint Boeing and NASA project announced in January 2023, the Sustainable Flight Demonstrator, is investigating a way to mitigate this issue while minimising drag and helping fuel efficiency.

The result is a Transonic Truss Braced Wing (TTBW) where struts connect a high-aspect ratio wing to the fuselage. A Boeing/NASA statement said a TTBW combined with engine, materials and systems advancements could cut fuel burn and emissions by up to 30% from today's most efficient single-aisle aircraft.

Bob Pearce, associate administrator for NASA's Aeronautics Research Mission Directorate, said the TTBW is a "transformative concept" with "a clear and viable path to informing the next generation of single-aisle aircraft."

A NASA Ames Research Center paper for the American Institute of Aeronautics and Astronautics noted that Northrop Grumman originally suggested a truss-braced wing for a long-range bomber.

NASA launched the Subsonic Ultra Green Aircraft Research project in 2009 to further study the concept, which led into research involving Boeing, General Electric, Georgia Tech, Virginia Tech, and NextGen Aeronautics.

A TTBW was later tested in the NASA Ames Research Center wind tunnel at Edwards Air Force Base, California.

A full-scale demonstrator aircraft known as the X-66A will test the truss-braced wing. In August 2023 the 24-year-old ex-Delta Air Lines McDonnell Douglas MD-90 (N931TB c/n 53532) was ferried across California from storage in Victorville to NASA's Palmdale facility at Edwards where it will undergo modification to become the testbed.

Flight testing was scheduled to start in 2028 from NASA's Armstrong Flight Research Center at Edwards. However, it was announced in April 2025 that the project has been paused "for later consideration" based on further configuration studies and testbed results. Boeing/NASA said their work had identified "the thin-wing concept as having broad applications for potential incorporation into aircraft with and without truss braces."

Rolls-Royce UltraFan

Engine-makers are working on a new generation of ultra-high-bypass ratio turbofans with advanced materials and gear-driven fan systems offering high propulsive and aerodynamic efficiencies and low noise.

The Rolls-Royce UltraFan demonstrator has a 140in fan opening, the widest on any civil aero engine ever developed. Rolls-Royce started static tests on the engine in spring 2023 in its Testbed 80 indoor aero-engine test chamber in Derby, the world's largest such facility, using 100% sustainable aviation fuel.

A Rolls-Royce statement said: "UltraFan has been a decade in the making, with the concept unveiled publicly in 2014. It is a fundamentally different design architecture as it incorporates a geared design that no other industry player has produced at this size before."

Key features include an Advance3 core combined with an ALECSys lean burn combustion system, a carbon-fibre composite casing and carbon-titanium fan blades.

Rolls-Royce says UltraFan will burn 25% less fuel than the company's first-generation Trent turbofan and be 10% more efficient than the Trent XWB on the A350.

CFM open rotor

At another engine supplier, CFM International, research into advanced engine architectures and combustion technologies is centred on the RISE (Revolutionary Innovation for Sustainable Engines) programme.

RISE is studying an open fan or open rotor architecture. Alternatively known

ABOVE • *JetZero disclosed its blended wing airliner concept in 2023.* JETZERO

BELOW • *Toulouse-based AURA AERO is working on the ERA small turboprop airliner called.* AURA AERO

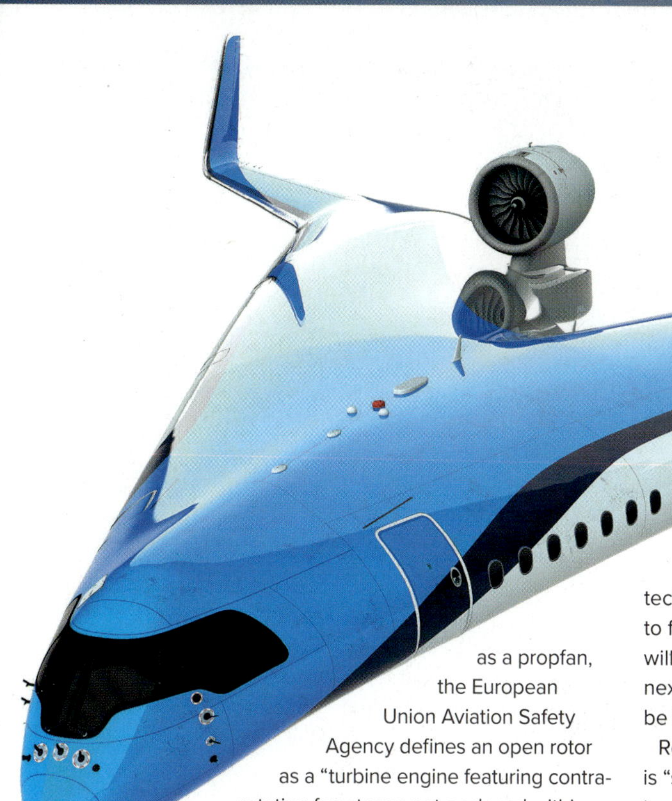

ABOVE • *KLM Royal Dutch Airlines supported TU Delft's Flying-V blended wing research project.* TU DELFT

as a propfan, the European Union Aviation Safety Agency defines an open rotor as a "turbine engine featuring contra-rotating fan stages not enclosed within a casing."

The RISE programme is also studying a compact core, thermal management, hybrid-electric systems, composite fan blades, heat-resistant metal alloys, ceramic matrix composites, additive manufacturing and full compatibility with sustainable aviation fuels and hydrogen.

Michel Brioude, vice president engineering and R&T at Safran Aircraft Engines (the 50/50 shareholder in CFM, with General Electric), in June 2023 reported "significant progress" to validate the design and start production on the first demonstrator parts.

Ground and flight tests will begin in the mid-2020s, with an open rotor demonstrator engine to be mounted on an Airbus A380 testbed. CFM aims to show the RISE technologies can cut fuel burn and carbon dioxide emissions by more than 20% compared to the company's

current-generation LEAP turbofan.

The RISE and UltraFan technologies are likely to find their way to future powerplants. CFM says RISE will "serve as the foundation for the next-generation CFM engine that could be available by the mid-2030s."

Rolls-Royce's marketing says UltraFan is "scalable, capable of being developed to create an engine with a thrust range of 25,000lb to more than 100,000lb, for narrowbody or widebody aircraft that may be developed from the 2030s."

Rolls-Royce adds UltraFan technologies could be applied to the company's current in-service engines to achieve efficiency and sustainability improvements in the nearer term. The company claims UltraFan "will also put us in the unique position of being able to offer a portfolio of two-shaft, three-shaft, direct drive and geared propulsion solutions to power future aircraft."

Electric dreams

Entirely new power sources for airliners are under investigation. Several organisations have explored hydrogen (see p.98). Electric/hybrid-electric power is the focus for other players.

NASA says electric technologies "offer innovative solutions to making

flight more sustainable – including lighter and more efficient motors, electronics and materials that can help reduce emission levels and improve fuel efficiency."

The US company magniX has developed a family of flight-proven electric propulsion units (EPU) and energy storage systems. In 2019 the Vancouver-based Harbour Air successfully test-flew the first all-electric commercial aircraft, the ePlane, a six-seat De Havilland DHC-2 Beaver retrofitted with a 750hp magni500 EPU. The first point-to-point ePlane test flight was in August 2022.

A system safety analysis on the engine and energy storage system installation is under way to meet regulators' reliability requirements. Harbour Air intends to fly an 'ePlane 2.0' in 2024. After battery requirements are harmonised certification of battery components is planned for 2025, the company said.

NASA, meanwhile, has its Electrified Powertrain Flight Demonstration (EPFD) which the agency says intends to "assist industry in addressing key technical barriers and risks associated with integrating electric systems into airliners, as well as help identify and evaluate new standards." The plan is to transition technologies into commercial products around 2030-2035.

The EPFD involves two flight demos using regional aircraft. GE Aerospace, Boeing and Aurora Flight Sciences will install an integrated, megawatt-class hybrid-electric propulsion system aboard a modified Saab 340B. Ground and flight trials are planned for the mid-2020s from Aurora Flight Sciences facilities. The other demo involves magniX working with AeroTEC and Air Tindi to test a hybrid powertrain on a modified De Havilland Dash 7 from the AeroTEC Flight Test Center in Moses Lake, Washington.

Germany's DLR has various electric aircraft projects including a gyrocopter, a general aviation aircraft called HyBird and H2ELECTRA, a fully-electric/hybrid-electric 50-seat turboprop airliner.

Heart ES-30

There is a growing crop of electric aircraft from start-up companies.

BELOW • *Eviation flew a prototype of its Alice all-electric aircraft in September 2022.* EVIATION

ABOVE • *Elfly is developing its NoEmi (No Emissions) seaplane to connect the fjords of Norway.* ELFLY

The now Los Angeles-based Heart Aerospace is working on the ES-30 offering 30 seats capacity and 200km range in all-electric configuration (400km in electric/hybrid or 800km in electric/hybrid with a lighter 25-passenger load).

Heart promises the ES-30, to be powered by four electric engines, will generate 50% less emissions (90% if sustainable aviation fuel is used), lower noise and what the company calls "significantly better" fuel, operating and maintenance costs compared to a current-generation turboprop.

Heart is working with BAE Systems to develop a "first-of-its-kind" lightweight battery for the ES-30 and Crane Aerospace & Electronics to define the aircraft's electrical power distribution system. Honeywell will provide the flight control system.

BELOW • *Heart Aerospace plans to deliver its ES-30 in 2029.* HEART AEROSPACE

Heart's marketing says the company's mission "is to create the world's greenest, most affordable and most accessible form of transport." The ES-30 has a struck a chord; there were orders for 250 ES-30s and purchase rights on 120 more at the time of writing in May 2025. Airlines including Air Canada, Icelandair and United Airlines have signed up. Heart plans two technology demonstrators, X1 and X2, before flying the ES-30. Service entry is planned for 2029.

Toulouse-based AURA AERO is working on a small turboprop airliner called ERA (Electric Regional Aircraft). Designed for passenger, business, cargo and medical evacuation missions, ERA will be powered by eight engines and carry 19 passengers or 1.9 tonnes of freight up to 900 nautical miles. Safran will supply the engines. First flight is planned for 2026 and service entry

in 2028. Letters of intent have been signed for several hundred aircraft.

Eviation flew a prototype of its Alice all-electric aircraft in September 2022. Powered by two magniX magni650 electric engines, Alice will be produced in three variants: nine-passenger commuter, six-passenger executive and all-cargo. The aircraft will have a 260kts cruise speed, 250nm range and up to 2,500lb payload.

Orders had passed 600 at the time of writing in May 2025, including from Air New Zealand, the US regional carriers Cape Air and Global Crossing, EVIA AERO in Germany and the UK lessor Monte. DHL Express has ordered the cargo variant.

Electra.aero is developing an electrically-powered short take-off and landing aircraft called the EL9 seating nine passengers which the company claims "will deliver the operational

ABOVE • *A Saab 340 and De Havilland Dash 7 are part of NASA's Electrified Powertrain Flight Demonstration.* NASA

BELOW • *Harbour Air test-flew the first all-electric commercial aircraft, the ePlane, in 2019.* HARBOUR AIR

flexibility of a helicopter with the safety and economics of a conventional fixed-wing aircraft." A technology demonstrator was unveiled in June 2023; its first flight is planned for 2025.

In June 2023 Elfly Aviation in Norway unveiled an all-electric commercial seaplane called NoEmi (No Emission) to be powered by two electric motors with up to 1MW combined output. NoEmi is designed for 200km journeys seating 19 passengers. Nine-seat business/executive, six-seat VIP and 13-seat tourist sightseeing configurations are also planned.

Elfly said it "intends to pursue an operator's certificate and bring the first aircraft into service, initially connecting the fjords of Norway" by 2030. Nordic Seaplanes and Loch Lomond Seaplanes has ordered the aircraft.

Limitations

As all these projects show, electric aircraft developments are focused on relatively small aircraft undertaking regional and commuter services.

A December 2021 blog by Air bp said: "Electric-powered flight will only be possible for short-haul journeys in the foreseeable future due to the weight of the batteries required."

The limitations led to one manufacturer, Tecnam, in June 2023 announcing it was pausing development of the P-Volt, a planned all-electric variant of its P2022 Traveller. The P-Volt had been due to enter service in 2026 with Norwegian carrier Widerøe but the Italian company said the technology "is not yet ripe."

A Tecnam statement explained: "The proliferation of aircraft with 'new' batteries would lead to unrealistic mission profiles that would quickly degrade after a few weeks of operation, making the all-electric passenger aircraft a mere 'green transition flagship' rather than a real player in the decarbonisation of aviation."

Tecnam continued: "Taking into account the most optimistic projections of slow charge cycles and the possible limitation of the maximum charge level per cycle, the real storage capacity would fall below 170Wh/kg, and only a few hundred flights would drive operators to replace the entire storage unit, with a dramatic increase in direct operating costs due to the reserves for battery replacement prices."

Fabio Russo, Tecnam's chief R&D officer, commented: "It has always been our culture to commit to achievable goals with customers and operators, and we intend to keep that promise. We hope that new technologies will make businesses viable sooner rather than later."

Electric aircraft developers remain confident the evolution will happen. Heart Aerospace, for instance, says future technology developments will extend the ES-30's range to 200km (or 400km hybrid) by the late 2020s, to 300km (500km hybrid) by the mid-2030s and 400km (600km hybrid) by the late 2030s.

Another developer, Maeve Aerospace, based in Delft in the Netherlands, is working on the design of a much larger fully-electric regional airliner,

now called the Maeve M80. Energy density of batteries on a system level is improving, Maeve Aerospace co-founder and CEO Jan Willem Heinen told this publication's editor in 2022.

Heinen said: "At 400kWh energy density at a system level we can fly 550km with 44 passengers. That's a serious mission. The energy density in 2023 is 450kWh at a system level. That's when you start making an impact and you start going for 60 passengers and 1,000km."

Sustainable aviation fuels

IATA said in one of its roadmaps the pace of electric/hybrid-electric (and hydrogen) development means "the only way to fully decouple the aviation demand growth curve from the emissions curve is to change the source of the carbon dioxide emissions: the fuel."

SAF provides a way for the industry to get on with decarbonising, an August 2022 Oliver Wyman consultancy report said: "A gallon [of SAF] can emit up to 80% less carbon dioxide than conventional jet fuel. [It] will be needed through much of this century."

There has been a noticeable ramp-up in activity on sustainable aviation fuel (SAF) early in the 2020s. Numerous airlines worldwide (including Lufthansa, United Airlines, Korean Air Lines, British Airways, Delta Air Lines, Ryanair, and Qantas Airways) have contracts to buy SAF. Infrastructure development is happening too, from a Fulcrum BioEnergy refinery at Stanlow in Cheshire to supply major UK airports to production facilities in North America, Australia, and the Middle East.

Considerable output increases are needed. IATA says around 125 million litres of SAF was produced in 2021 but it says a production capacity of 449 billion litres per year is required by 2050. A near-term target is to achieve 2.7 billion tonnes in 2025.

Feedstocks

There are two types of SAF – biofuels (made from biomass such as oilseed crops, agricultural and forestry residues, or municipal/industrial waste streams) and synthetic fuels (alternatively called eSAFs or 'e-kerosene') produced using chemical synthesis.

An agency called ASTM international approves biofuels' use as 'drop in' fuels blended with conventional Jet A1. Biofuels were used for the various SAF demonstration flights undertaken by some airlines and manufacturers in the 2000s/2010s.

There are downsides to sustainable aviation fuels. Luisa Barnes, an analyst at the IBA consultancy, wrote in an August 2023 report: "The cultivation, harvesting, storage and transportation processes involved and the indirect land use change impacts during extraction and production of certain SAF feedstocks will result in greenhouse gas emission release and have detrimental environmental consequences."

IATA pointed out it is "an absolute requirement" to produce aviation fuels using 'green' energy (using renewable power rather than fossil fuels), but the International Energy Agency estimates global electricity demand could be 75%-150% higher than today by mid-century, with aviation accounting for 20% of total electricity production requirements.

IATA reflected: "This gives a sense of the magnitude of the infrastructure that will be needed globally to generate and connect renewable energy to grids, production sites and households – and for aviation to airports and aircraft."

ABOVE • *Electra.aero is developing an electrically-powered short take-off and landing aircraft seating nine passengers.* ELECTRA.AERO

BELOW • *A joint NASA/Boeing product is converting an MD-90 to a testbed for truss-braced wings.* NASA

AI in the sky

In 2023 artificial intelligence (AI) and debate about its consequences for humanity – good or bad – has been prominent on the news agenda.

AI is a field of computer science defined as machines and systems doing tasks that typically only humans had the intelligence to perform, including reasoning and problem-solving, knowledge representation, planning, learning, processing, and perception. A subset of AI is machine learning, where systems analyse data to automatically detect complex patterns and 'learn' information.

AI has become part of everyday life – from customised content and automatic recommendations on the web to apps that understand human speech. The rise of AI, together with advances in computational power and data storage, means data can today be collected and analysed on an industrial scale.

Today's connected commercial aircraft and engines generate more than 30 times the amount of data of previous-generation aircraft, the Oliver Wyman consultancy estimates. There is all the data commercial aviation generates at every level – from air traffic management to maintenance, repair, and overhaul, to airline IT systems and airport operations. By 2026 the aviation industry will generate 98 billion gigabytes annually, Oliver Wyman predicts. No wonder aerospace is enthusiastically embracing artificial intelligence.

Manufacturers have brought out advanced analytics to help customers more effectively understand their data in operational decision-making. Products such as Airbus Skywise and Boeing AnalytX integrate data from aircraft and post-flight reports and maintenance information. Operators can check the reliability of individual systems and components to seek problems. Predictive modelling identifies upcoming maintenance interruptions and efficiency opportunities.

Rolls-Royce has the Intelligent Borescope, an industry-first AI engine inspection tool generating 3-D colour images of objects as large as turbine blades. Engines work hard (an average aircraft does 20,000 flights in its lifetime) and with many parts to track (typically around 20,000 components), Intelligent Borescope is designed to speed up inspections and improve data capture and analysis.

AI is even beginning to make its presence felt for passengers. Collins Aerospace's InteliSence tracks interactions between passengers' personal electronic devices and objects within an aircraft cabin. Information is shared with cabin crew, who can use it proactively to offer specific items for passengers, like a coffee cup refill for example.

Early forays into AI at airports were centred on biometrics for security. Devin Liddell, principal futurist at Teague design consultancy, says AI could comprehend which passengers are at the gate and which are not, the bags they have and the other people they're travelling with, and even how they physically move around an airport.

Operations

With the waiting times for sustainable fuels to scale up and new-generation aircraft and engines to arrive, the industry is seeking savings by other means.

IATA said in its operations roadmap: "Efficiency in air traffic management results in reduced fuel burn and for every tonne of fuel saved, 3.16 tonnes of carbon dioxide emissions are abated. It is imperative that all stakeholders find solutions to deliver these efficiencies, many of which are recognised as being achievable in the near term."

Examples of air traffic management innovations include continuous descent and climb trajectories enabling pilots to follow a flexible and optimum flight profile, and free route airspace – where, as its name implies, operators fly preferred routes between waypoints without being constrained by fixed airspace structures.

Air navigation services provider NATS introduced the first free route airspace in the UK in March 2023 as part of the West Airspace Deployment covering 54,000 square miles of airspace over Wales and southwest England.

At the same time, NATS introduced 'systemisation' in the airspace between 7,000ft and 24,500. NATS explains: "By using the latest aircraft technology and approach to airspace design thinking, a systemised network has highly defined flight paths which use the available airspace as efficiently as possible."

Quantum

The technology push in aerospace goes to the frontier of engineering – including artificial intelligence (see panel) and even quantum computing, a new

In an October 2022 report, S&P cited other challenges around SAFs: "Favourable pricing, feedstock certainty and availability, as well as the willingness of governments and regulators to provide incentives."

In a 2022 statement, IATA urged policymakers to provide support to boost supply and minimise costs:

"Electricity production through solar or wind power faced similar hurdles as these technologies replaced fossil fuels. With effective policy incentives, both are now affordable and widely available." In September 2023 the UK Department for Transport announced a 'revenue certainty' scheme to encourage SAF investment.

RIGHT • *CFM International's RISE programme is researching an open rotor, among other technologies.* CFM INTERNATIONAL

breed of high-performance computers more sophisticated than the most powerful supercomputers around today.

'Quantum' refers to how so-called quantum particles can be in two places at the same time. Nobel Laureate Richard Feynman proposed quantum computing in 1981 and technology giants including Microsoft and Google have explored it over the past 20 years.

Rolls-Royce is interested in this emerging field. In a February 2023 blog, Professor Leigh Lapworth, a Rolls-Royce Fellow in Computational Science, wrote: "High performance computing is critical to our business and its impact extends across the life of our products…Yet there are still things we don't and can't yet model."

Lapworth said: "We have an ambition to model an entire gas turbine in high fidelity and new systems…These are calculations that require thousands of times more computing resources than we currently use and would take many months to complete on even the most powerful of today's high-performance computers."

Lapworth highlighted the advantages: "Whole-engine calculations that take months could be completed in days or even hours. This means faster results, which means a faster design, huge reductions in testing and development costs and even better products that are faster to market."

Airbus is exploring quantum applications with experts from academia and start-ups. It says: "We strongly believe quantum computing, in tandem with more traditional high-performance computing solutions, can help us to solve key computationally intensive tasks."

Fresh thinking

Back to the aircraft. Research institution Bauhaus Luftfahrt in Germany (the name calls back to the famous Bauhaus art and design school) has come up with several novel ideas.

Its CityBird aircraft concept features aft-mounted engines, a small and faired landing gear, and a high-lift system along the entire span of the wing. The Ce-Liner with 189 seats features two ducted fans and a 'self-trimming' wing using morphing techniques to constantly adapt its shape to varying flight conditions.

A separate concept, the Propulsive Fuselage, has conventional wing-mounted turbofan engines powering electrical generators driving smaller motors and fans to improve efficiency and reduce energy use.

IATA said in one of its roadmaps that airframe/engine innovations "become gradually more expensive and more difficult to achieve over time, as interdependencies start cancelling out theoretical benefits."

For example, the association said, although high-aspect wings could improve energy efficiency they could

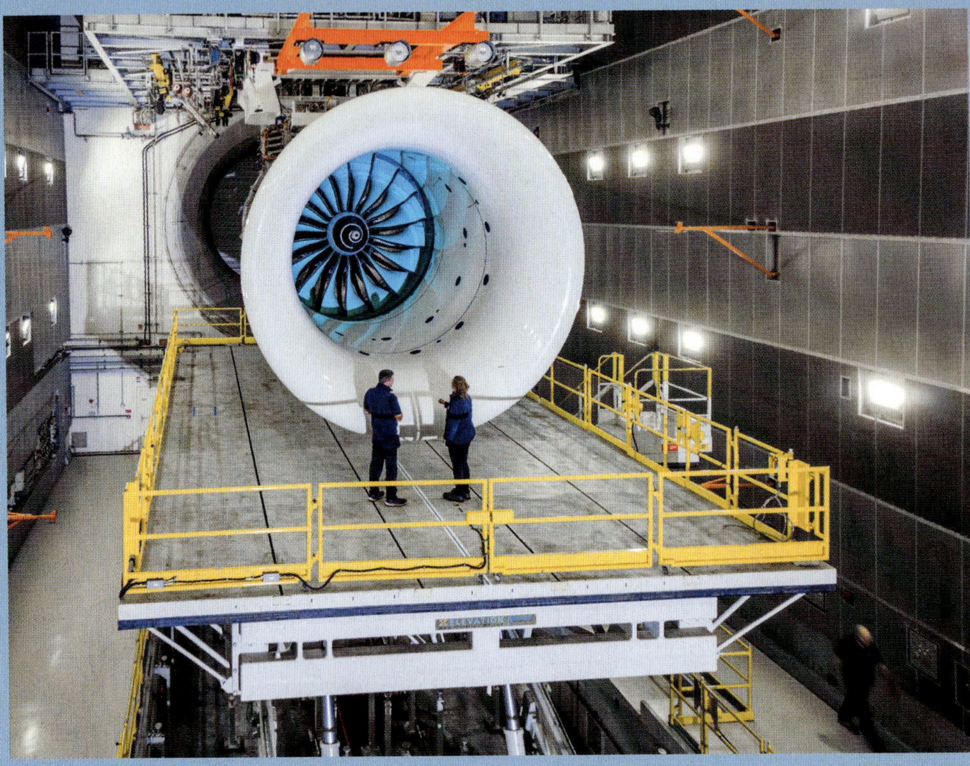

ABOVE • *Rolls-Royce ran its new UltraFan demonstrator engine in its huge Testbed 80 facility in Derby in 2023.* ULTRAFAN

be heavier, requiring larger engines to achieve the same take-off, climb and cruise performance.

And IATA said: "Ultra-high bypass ratio engines could theoretically provide a lower specific fuel consumption, but the extra drag and weight of the engine, and the associated cascade effects on the mass of the entire aircraft, could cancel these benefits."

This is encouraging exploration into entirely different ways of doing things from the proven 'tube and wing' configuration of a conventional aircraft. The natural world is providing inspiration.

Biomimicry, broadly defined as the emulation of models, systems, and elements of nature for the purpose of solving human problems, has influenced various engineering developments over the years. Kingfishers inspired the shape of the bullet train, geckos the functionality of adhesives and whales

BELOW • *Germany's Bauhaus Luftfahrt has proposed a Ce-Liner with 189 seats and two ducted fans.* BAUHAUS LUFTFAHRT

ABOVE • Air navigation services providers say modernising airspace is one near-term way to improve efficiency. NATS

the shape of wind turbine blades, to give a few examples.

In aerospace, in 2019 Airbus presented Bird of Prey, a concept 80-seat hybrid-electric regional turboprop aircraft mimicking the wing and tail structure of an eagle or falcon, with individually-controlled 'feathers' and a split tail for control. Airbus emphasised Bird of Prey's purpose was to inspire young aerospace engineers, but it said the radical concept was "grounded in reality."

Another bio-inspired Airbus demonstrator, AlbatrossONE, was a small remote-controlled aircraft with wings that could freely 'flap' in flight. A hinge enabled the wings to lock for long-distance soaring and unlock for manoeuvring in wind gusts or turbulence, just as a seabird's do. The idea was to create a flexible wing, reducing loads

and the need for heavily-reinforced wings, reducing overall weight.

Blended wing body

An especially striking future aircraft concept is the blended wing body (BWB). This smooths, or blends, a fuselage upwards into the wing, with the cabin, cargo hold, and fuel tanks integrated into a single structure and the engines mounted high on the rear fuselage – a significant design difference from the conventional tube and wing.

A BWB configuration enables the entire aircraft to generate lift, which minimises drag, helps fuel economy, and creates areas for carrying large payloads (cargo or passenger) in the central body of the aircraft.

The BWB concept is not new (research into it can be traced as far back as the

1920s) and its most famous application is the US Air Force B-2 Spirit 'stealth bomber'. With its advantages for efficiency, research has stepped up.

Building on research work carried out in the 1990s with McDonnell Douglas and Boeing when they were separate companies ahead of their 1999 merger, NASA worked with Boeing's Phantom Works division in the 2000s to explore BWB designs. The result was the pair Boeing X-48 subscale uncrewed aerial vehicles (built, incidentally, in the UK by Cranfield Aerospace Solutions).

The X-48 flight testing, carried out early in the 2010s at the-then NASA Dryden (now Armstrong) Flight Research Center, focused on the low-speed, low-altitude flight characteristics of the BWB, including engine-out control, stall characteristics and handling qualities. Boeing and NASA also undertook research using subscale BWB models in the wind tunnels at the NASA Langley Research Center in Virginia.

The X-48 tests were part of NASA's Environmentally Responsible Aviation programme, a research and development initiative investigating technologies to improve fuel efficiency, lower noise and reduce emissions. (In NASA, the blended wing body is also known as a Hybrid Wing-Body or HWB.)

Another BWB research concept is the Flying-V from TU Delft in the Netherlands, which KLM Royal Dutch Airlines has supported. At 55m in length with a 65m wingspan and

BELOW • Recent years have seen increased activity in the industry around sustainable aviation fuels. BOEING

capacity for 314 passengers, Flying-V would have the same wingspan, passenger capacity and cargo volume as the Airbus A350-900.

TU Delft says the Flying-V is designed with current-generation turbofan engines in mind while also being adaptable for future electric or hybrid-electric engines, and that the aerodynamic shape and reduced weight will mean it uses 20% less fuel than an A350-900.

TU Delft has conducted wind tunnel testing campaigns into the Flying-V's aerodynamics, structure, airframe-engine integration, cabin design and expected flight characteristics. Data has been acquired through balance measurements and flow visualisation techniques to study specific aerodynamic characteristics such as stability, angle of attack and lift-to-drag ratio.

Other organisations are working on blended wings. Bombardier Aerospace announced in 2023 that it has tested a scale demonstrator for its EcoJet R&D project investigating new technologies. Airbus is studying the BWB as part of its ZEROe programme; the company previously undertook test flights using a scaled demonstrator called MAVERIC.

In August 2023 a start-up US company, JetZero, announced plans to fly a full-scale BWB demonstrator by 2027. A JetZero statement said the company "is collaborating with Northrop Grumman and Scaled Composites, who bring extensive experience in advanced aircraft design, manufacturing and mission systems integration to build and test the full-scale demonstrator."

Jet Zero has selected Pratt & Whitney geared turbofan engines to power the demonstrator. Pratt & Whitney GATORWORKS is supporting JetZero with design and integration of the propulsion system.

JetZero has received US Department of Defense Innovation Unit funding, but the company said a BWB's reduced fuel consumption, emissions and noise is promising for a future airliner variant as well as a military aircraft.

JetZero chief executive officer Tom O'Leary said: "The BWB is the best first step on the path to zero carbon emissions. It offers 50% lower fuel burn using today's engines and the airframe efficiency needed to support a transition to zero carbon emissions propulsion in the future. No other proposed aircraft comes close in terms of efficiency."

'People want to fly'

It remains to be seen exactly if and when a blended wing body makes it to commercial flight – and exactly how the various technologies mentioned in this article take their place in the industry.

Whether they are developing an entirely new product or modernising those already in service, a manufacturer must ensure their product satisfies regulatory and safety criteria. They must also convince industry decision-makers and investors. Tube-and-wing has persisted in the industry because it is practical, established, and cost-effective.

Looking ahead, the complex web of factors surrounding civil aviation – economics, technology, politics, and culture – will continue to shape civil aviation in numerous ways, just as they have over the last century. Other forces, principally the environment, social change, and demographic shifts, are likely to exert their own forces too.

Change is the one constant of our world, as the first two decades of the 21st century showed. Sat on the edge of tomorrow, aerospace will have to adapt – but commercial airliners seemingly have an assured role.

There will always be a requirement to speedily move people and goods. The distances may vary from between continents or just a few hundred miles, but the need for air transport will continue.

Above all, Airbus remarked in its 2023 Global Market Forecast, "people want to fly."

ABOVE • *Airbus 'Bird of Prey' concept, an example of research into how biomimicry might work in aviation.* AIRBUS

BELOW • *Maeve Aerospace is one of numerous companies working on electric airliner concepts.* MAEVE AEROSPACE